A HIGH PERFORMANCE ARCHITECTURE FOR PROLOG

**THE KLUWER INTERNATIONAL SERIES
IN ENGINEERING AND COMPUTER SCIENCE**

PARALLEL PROCESSING AND
FIFTH GENERATION COMPUTING

Consulting Editor

Doug DeGroot

Other books in the series:

PARALLEL EXECUTION OF LOGIC PROGRAMS
John S. Conery ISBN 0–89838–194–0

PARALLEL COMPUTATION AND COMPUTERS FOR
ARTIFICIAL INTELLIGENCE
Janusz S. Kowalik ISBN 0–89838–227–0

MEMORY STORAGE PATTERNS IN PARALLEL PROCESSING
Mary E. Mace ISBN 0–89838–239–4

SUPERCOMPUTER ARCHITECTURE
Paul B. Schneck ISBN 0–89838–234–4

ASSIGNMENT PROBLEMS IN PARALLEL
AND DISTRIBUTED COMPUTING
Shahid H. Bokhari ISBN 0–89838–240–8

MEMORY PERFORMANCE OF PROLOG ARCHITECTURES
Evan Tick ISBN 0–89838–254–8

DATABASE MACHINES AND KNOWLEDGE BASE MACHINES
Masaru Kitsuregawa ISBN 0–89838–257–2

PARALLEL PROGRAMMING AND COMPILERS
Constantine D. Polychronopoulos ISBN 0–89838–288–2

ANALYSIS OF CACHE PERFORMANCE FOR OPERATING
SYSTEMS AND MULTIPROGRAMMING
Anant Agarwal ISBN 0–7923–9005–9

DATA ORGANIZATION IN PARALLEL COMPUTERS
H.A.G. Wijshoff ISBN 0–89838–304–8

A HIGH PERFORMANCE ARCHITECTURE FOR PROLOG

by

T.P. Dobry
University of Hawaii at Manoa

KLUWER ACADEMIC PUBLISHERS
Boston/Dordrecht/London

Distributors for North America:
Kluwer Academic Publishers
101 Philip Drive
Assinippi Park
Norwell, Massachusetts 02061 USA

Distributors for all other countries:
Kluwer Academic Publishers Group
Distribution Centre
Post Office Box 322
3300 AH Dordrecht, THE NETHERLANDS

Library of Congress Cataloging-in-Publication Data

Dobry, T. P., 1953–
   A high performance architecture for PROLOG / by T.P. Dobry.
      p.   cm. — (The Kluwer international series in engineering and
computer science ; SECS 90. Parallel processing and fifth generation
computing)
   Includes bibliographical references.
   ISBN 0-7923-9060-1
   1. Prolog (Computer program language)   2. Computer architecture.
I. Title.   II. Series: Kluwer international series in engineering
and computer science ; SECS 90.   III. Series: Kluwer international
series in engineering and computer science. Parallel processing and
fifth generation computing.
QA76.73.P76D63   1990
006.3—dc20   89–26725
                                                        CIP

Copyright © 1990 by Kluwer Academic Publishers

Printed in the United States of America

TABLE OF CONTENTS

CHAPTER 1 INTRODUCTION 1
LOGIC PROGRAMMING 2
A PROLOG MODEL 3
    Some Example Applications in Prolog. 10
    Progress in Prolog Implementations. 11
COMPUTER ARCHITECTURE 14
OTHER SYMBOLIC COMPUTING PROCESSORS 15
    The Japanese PSI. 16
    The LISP Machines. 16
    The SPUR Project. 18
MOTIVATION 19
CONTRIBUTIONS 21
ORGANIZATION 21
CHAPTER 2 AN ABSTRACT PROLOG MACHINE   23
DATA TYPES 23
MEMORY AREAS 25
SOME DEFINITIONS 30
INSTRUCTION SET 32
    Procedure Code. 32
    Indexing Code. 36
    Clause Code. 39
    Data Manipulation Code. 42
    An Example of Compiled Code. 47
FUNDAMENTAL OPERATIONS 49
    Failure. 49
    Variable Binding and Dereferencing. 50
    Trailing. 56
    General Unification. 58

CHAPTER SUMMARY 59
CHAPTER 3 A MODIFIED WAM 61
ADDRESS SPACE OF THE PLM 63
    Representing Data. 64
    Representing Code. 71
COMPLETING THE INSTRUCTION SET 74
    Support for cdr-coding. 74
    The cut Operation. 78
    An Unnecessary Instruction. 86
ENHANCEMENTS TO THE WAM 87
    The Environment Size. 87
    Indexing Instructions. 88
    An Unnecessary Register. 94
    Tail Recursion Revisited. 95
IMPLEMENTING BUILT-IN FUNCTIONS 105
    Compiler Implemented Built-ins. 105
    Internal Built-ins. 107
    External Built-ins. 107
    Some Particularly Difficult Built-ins. 109
        Side-effect Variables. 109
        General assert and retract - Overview. 111
        Code Space Modification. 117
CHAPTER SUMMARY 123
CHAPTER 4 THE ARCHITECTURE BECOMES A
    MACHINE 125
THE PREFETCH UNIT 126
DEFINING A BASIC DATA PATH 130
DEFINING A MICROENGINE 133
TUNING THE DATA PATH AND THE MICROCODE 140
THE PATH TO MEMORY 146
    Write Buffering. 148
    Choice Point Cache. 149

Environment and Trail Buffering. 151
CHAPTER SUMMARY 153
CHAPTER 5   THE EXPERIMENT 155
METHODOLOGY 155
THE SIMULATORS 157
    ISA Simulation - Level 1. 157
    RTL Simulation - Level 2. 158
THE BENCHMARK SET 160
RESULTS 161
    Determinate concat - A Case Study. 161
    The Effects of cdr-coding. 168
    The Effects of Environment Trimming. 175
    The Effects of Sidetracking. 178
    The Effects of Host and Memory Speed. 181
    The Effects of Buffers and Caches. 186
    A Critique of the PLM Microcode. 190
FURTHER IMPROVEMENTS TO THE PLM 196
CHAPTER SUMMARY 199
CHAPTER 6   CONCLUSIONS 201
DIRECTIONS FOR FUTURE RESEARCH 203
CONCLUSIONS 205
BIBLIOGRAPHY 207
INDEX 215

LIST OF FIGURES

Figure 1.1: Prolog Program Structure. 5

Figure 1.2: AND/OR Search Tree 7

Figure 1.3: A Prolog Example. 8

Figure 1.4: Search Tree for grandparent Database 9

Figure 1.5: A Simple Machine Simulator 12

Figure 1.6: Symbolic Differentiation 13

Figure 2.1: Structure Representation 24

Figure 2.2: List Representation 26

Figure 2.3: Code Space Organization 27

Figure 2.4: Data Space Configuration 28

Figure 2.5: An OR Node 33

Figure 2.6: Stack Snapshot 35

Figure 2.7: Typical Procedure Code 37

Figure 2.8: OR Node with Indexing Instructions 39

Figure 2.9: Last Call Optimization 41

Figure 2.10: A Complete AND Node 43

Figure 2.11: Prolog Code for grandparent 47

Figure 2.12: Compiled Code for grandparent 48

Figure 2.13: Variable Binding Strategies 52

Figure 2.14: A Reference Chain of length 2 54

Figure 2.15: Binding Heap and Stack variables 55

Figure 2.16: The Stack for Trailing Variables 57

Figure 3.1: Block Diagram of a PLM System 62

Figure 3.2: The PLM Instruction Set 63

Figure 3.3: PLM Data Types. 65

Figure 3.4: Structure Based Representation. 67

Figure 3.5: List Based Representation. 68

Figure 3.6: Cdr-Coded Representation. 69

Figure 3.7: A More Complex List Represented 70

Figure 3.8: Instruction Formats. 72

Figure 3.9: Opcode Assignment. 73

Figure 3.10: Instruction Sequences 76

Figure 3.11: A Snapshot of the Stack. 81

Figure 3.12: Constant Block Code. 91

Figure 3.13: Code for append 97

Figure 3.14: Search Tree Diagram for append 98

Figure 3.15: Code for Sidetracking append 99

Figure 3.16: Search Tree Diagram for Sidetracking append 100

Figure 3.17: Compiled Code for nsplit 103

Figure 3.18: A Problem Unifying Compiled Code. 113

Figure 3.19: Structure Representation of a Clause. 114

Figure 3.20: Prolog Database Procedures. 115

Figure 3.21: Source database for concat 116

Figure 3.22: Example builtin code. 117

Figure 3.23: Using Asserta 120

Figure 3.24: Using Assertz. 121

Figure 4.1: PLM Data Path. 131

Figure 4.2: MicroEngine. 134

Figure 4.3: Selecting Tags for Branching. 142

Figure 4.4: MDR Register. 143

Figure 4.5: Tags in the ALU. 145

Figure 5.1: Compiled code for concat. 163

Figure 5.2: Compiling concat with sidetracking 164

Figure 5.3: Explicit copying concat 165

Figure 5.4: List Copy concat 167

Figure 5.5: Performance vs Memory Access Time 184

Figure 5.6: Performance vs Host Speed 187

LIST OF TABLES

Table 1.1: Comparison with Warren Results 20

Table 5.1: Summary of concat Performance 168

Table 5.2: Multi-element List Unification 170

Table 5.3: Single Element List Processing 172

Table 5.4: Corrected Cdr-coding Microcode 175

Table 5.5: The Effects of Environment Trimming 176

Table 5.6: The Effects of sidetracking 178

Table 5.7: Sidetracking Memory and Instruction Data(%) 180

Table 5.8: Memory Reference Behavior 182

Table 5.9: The Effects of Memory Access Time 183

Table 5.10: The Effect of Host Speed 186

Table 5.11: The Effects of Buffers and Caches 188

Table 5.12: The Effect of the Prefetch Unit 191

Table 5.13: Static Microcode Statistics 192

Table 5.14: Dynamic Bus Utilization 195

Table 5.15: ICC and Dynamic Memory Statistics 196

Table 5.16: MEMDAT bus Utilization 198

Table 6.1: Comparison with Warren's results 206

PREFACE

Artificial Intelligence is entering the mainstream of computer applications and as techniques are developed and integrated into a wide variety of areas they are beginning to tax the processing power of conventional architectures. To meet this demand, specialized architectures providing support for the unique features of symbolic processing languages are emerging. The goal of the research presented here is to show that an architecture specialized for Prolog can achieve a ten-fold improvement in performance over conventional, general-purpose architectures. This book presents such an architecture for high performance execution of Prolog programs.

The architecture is based on the abstract machine description introduced by David H.D. Warren known as the Warren Abstract Machine (WAM). The execution model of the WAM is described and extended to provide a complete Instruction Set Architecture (ISA) for Prolog known as the PLM. This ISA is then realized in a microarchitecture and finally in a hardware design. The work described here represents one of the first efforts to implement the WAM model in hardware. The approach taken is that of direct implementation of the high level WAM instruction set in hardware resulting in a CISC style architecture.

The design of the PLM is described at many levels. First, at the language level, some of the features of Prolog are discussed, particularly as they relate to their implementation at the ISA level. For Prolog, the unique fundamental operations of unification and backtracking provide the opportunity for specialized support to achieve high performance. The instruction set of the WAM provides for compiled unification in Prolog programs and provides a mechanism for backtracking. This book proposes a variation on backtracking, called sidetracking, for more efficient implementation in many instances. The ISA enhancements to the WAM are then described. Next, the design of the microarchitecture is discussed with emphasis on those features providing special support for the ISA. These include parallel internal data paths, support for tagged data, and memory buffers and caches to support operations specified in the ISA. Finally, to complete the experiment of the PLM, the microarchitecture was realized in physical hardware. This hardware validated the decisions made at each stage of the design. This important step in the experiment shows that the design features discussed here can indeed be realized in physical hardware and achieve the desired performance. In addition, simulators were written and utilized at each stage to measure and study the design with the hardware providing feedback to make the simulators more realistic. A quantitative analysis of the design features of the PLM is provided based on the results of these simulator studies. These results show that a ten-fold performance advantage is indeed achieved over the Prolog implementation proposed by Warren for a general-purpose processor. Directions for future study to further improve the performance of the PLM are also provided.

The work described here was done with the support of many people, principle amoung these was Professor Alvin Despain, for the years of support and encouragement that made this work enjoyable. He introduced me to Prolog and the WAM and provided many hours of discussion and advice which made this research possible. I would also like to thank Professor Yale Patt who provided many useful insights into microarchitecture design.

I am grateful to all of the members of the Aquarius Berkeley group, particularly Robert Yung, Barry Fagin, and Jung-Herng Chang who assisted in bringing the PLM hardware to reality. I would also like to acknowledge the help of Mike Kates of Westinghouse Electric Corporation for his contributions in the early stages of the hardware design and Peter Van Roy for his insights and the PLM compiler.

Thanks also to Andrea Pappas for help in preparing this manuscript. Finally, I am indebted to the staff at Xenologic Incorporated, and in particular Bart Sano, for many hours of discussion on some of the ideas presented here and for the opportunity to test those ideas in hardware.

Tep Dobry
University of Hawaii

A HIGH PERFORMANCE ARCHITECTURE FOR PROLOG

CHAPTER 1

INTRODUCTION

In the Tenth Turing Lecture, Allen Newell and Herbert Simon state that "Symbols lie at the root of intelligent action..." [43]. To design and produce intelligent computing systems, it follows that systems capable of processing symbols are required. Such computers will adhere to a model of computation based on what Newell and Simon term formal symbol systems. The intent in this book is to develop the principles by which high performance symbolic processors can be designed.

Computers have traditionally been viewed as "number crunching" devices. However, since the early days of computing their capability to store and retrieve vast quantities of symbolic information has been exploited in a wide variety of application areas, for example in payroll and financial transaction processing. The early uses of computers in these areas consisted of manipulation and storage of symbolic data with the analysis and decision processes remaining with the user. With the growth of the field of Artificial Intelligence, the trend has been to automate decision making and the analysis of symbolic data, thus using computers to process symbols as well as manipulate them. To write programs for this type of processing, specialized languages have been developed such as LISP [38], SNOBOL [26], and Prolog [14], whose fundamental operations deal with symbols rather than numbers. With these languages running on conventional architectures it has been found that symbolic computing can be a very time consuming process.

Many of the problems to which computing power is applied today are largely symbolic in nature. Examples include systems for natural language processing, knowledge representation, expert advising, theorem proving and algebraic manipulation. An even larger class of problems may be attacked symbolically to direct the flow of numeric operations. This is especially important, for example, in Computer Aided Design. The Aquarius Project [17, 19], of which this research is a part, proposes a computer architecture consisting of a heterogeneous collection of processing elements, some dedicated to numeric operations and others directed at symbolic operations.

The research presented here investigates the types of architectural features required for efficient symbolic calculations. Specifically, an architecture for executing Prolog programs is proposed with the goal of improving the performance by an order of magnitude over conventional architectures.

LOGIC PROGRAMMING - A Paradigm for Symbolic Computing

Early work in symbolic processing was hampered by the nature of programming languages geared only toward numeric (scientific) calculations. The first major breakthrough came in 1960 with the advent of LISP invented by John McCarthy [39]. In LISP, the fundamental data item is not a number but an atom (i.e. a symbol). Lisp provides a uniform mechanism for organizing data items into lists and a collection of fundamental operations for defining and manipulating lists and describing their use as functions. LISP is based on a mathematical formalism - the Lambda Calculus of Church [12]. LISP has gained wide popularity particularly for artificial intelligent applications.

Another formal symbol system - logic - has been studied and employed since the time of the ancient Greeks. At the heart of many modern computing systems for logic is the Resolution Principle described by Robinson [50]. This principle describes an efficient formal system for carrying forth reasoning for theorem proving systems. The next step was Green's [25] idea of problem solving via theorem proving. The ideas of Robinson and Green were carried toward a computational model by Kowalski [34]. Here a subset of the first order predicate calculus is restricted in form to Horn clauses (without loss of generality), and shown to be useful as a programming language. This work was further refined resulting in the implementation of a programming language based on logic by Colmerauer [14] in Marseille in about 1972, namely Prolog. Prolog stands for PROgramming in LOGic and is an implementation of Horn clause logic [35]. Prolog has gained widespread popularity in Europe and has been chosen as the kernel language of the Japanese Fifth Generation Computer Project [24]. It is becoming recognized and more popular in this country.

Prolog is a general purpose programming language with single assignments to variables. It can be shown that Prolog is a Turing equivalent language, i.e. that any computable function (computable by a Turing Machine) can be computed by Prolog. Prolog describes algorithms in terms of a logic component and a control component [36]. In general, the logic component is provided by the programmer and the control component is provided by the total hardware and software system. In particular, mechanisms for unification and backtracking, are defined by the language.

A PROLOG MODEL

A logic program consists of a collection of statements of what is known to be true by the system. The program is used by posing a query to ask if some other statement is true based on this knowledge. The statements in the program take two forms - facts and rules. A fact states that a relation holds or that a predicate is true for the data specified in the statement. A rule says that for some relation to hold for some data, certain other relations must be shown to hold. For example, the statement

$$f(0,0).$$

says that the relation **f** holds for 0 and 0. The statement

$$f(N,F) <-- g(N,X),h(X,F).$$

says that the relation **f** holds for any data items represented by the variables N and F *IF* the relation **g** holds for N and X *AND* the relation **h** holds for X and F. This is the declarative interpretation of a logic program. The statement may also be read procedurally; namely, in order to show **f** holds for N and F, one must first show that **g** holds for N and X and then that **h** holds for X and F.

As a programming language, Prolog retains the declarative and procedural semantics of logic programming but is executed procedurally. To execute a program, Prolog adds control semantics to the logic specification to provide an algorithm to arrive at the solution to a query. This use of logic as a programming language was first described by Kowalski [36] and is summarized by him as:

$$Algorithm = Logic + Control$$

Figure 1.1 shows a static view of a Prolog program. The collection of statements is called the *database*. The statements are grouped into *procedures* based on the predicate or relation. The statements are called *clauses*. A clause has a *head* (or goal) and a *body* consisting of procedure calls (subgoals). If the body is empty, the clause is a fact. The head has a predicate (or functor) and a set of arguments (which can be empty).

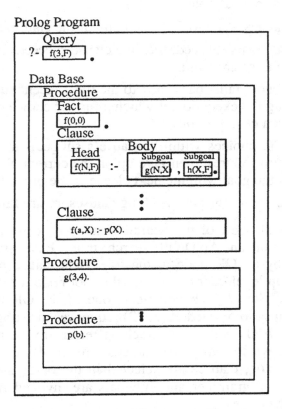

Figure 1.1: Prolog Program Structure.

The control semantics provided by Prolog implement a depth first search over the solution space defined by the program. This search strategy is executed by recursive application of the following steps. Given a goal (query):

(1)   Find the first clause in the program which has a matching

predicate and whose arguments will *unify* with the goal. Unification is a matching process which will generally bind some variables.

(2)   Invoke each subgoal, of the body of the clause, as a goal.

-If all subgoals succeed, then the clause succeeds and all variable bindings are valid.

-If a subgoal fails, backtrack to the most recent subgoal visited during the execution at which a further choice exists (indicated by a *choice-point*).

-If all the choices within a clause's subgoals are exhausted (i.e. return failure), then give up on the current clause and try to unify the goal with the next clause in the procedure.

-If there are no further matching clauses, return failure.

A dynamic view of this search strategy is seen in Figure 1.2 in the form of an AND/OR search tree. Each procedure is represented by an OR node in the tree, each clause by an AND node. The top level query identifies the root node for the problem being posed. Step (1) above selects one of the OR branches to identify a clause to be tried. Step (2) sequences the subgoals of the clause in the AND node. Backtracking returns to the most recent OR node for which additional choices remain. By convention in sequential Prolog, clauses are selected in the order they are provided by the programmer and subgoals are invoked from left to right within a clause.

The declarative semantics of a Prolog program provides a great deal of flexibility to the programmer in the use of Prolog procedures. For example, the program in Figure 1.3 shows two procedures, *grandparent*, describing a rule for determining if the grandparent relation holds between two individuals, and the *parent* procedure which is a collection of facts describing pairs for whom the parent relation holds. (Note: by convention, variables begin with upper case letters and symbols begin with lower case). The grandparent clause states that X is the grandparent of Y if there is a

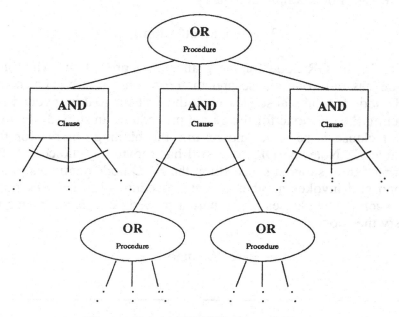

Figure 1.2: AND/OR Search Tree

Z such that Z is the parent of Y and X is the parent of Z. With these two procedures, queries may be posed in several forms:

(1)   grandparent(A,tom)? asking for a grandparent of tom.

(2)   grandparent(paul,B)? asking for a grandchild of paul.

(3)   grandparent(alice,tom)? asking if alice is the grandparent of tom.

(4)   grandparent(X,Y)? asking for any pairs X and Y known to the database for whom the grandparent relation holds. Through backtracking this query form will provide all such

pairs.

The program of Figure 1.3 is shown in the AND/OR tree of Figure 1.4. For example, the query

?- grandparent(A,tom).

begins in the OR node for the grandparent procedure. This procedure has only one clause and therefore only one branch to the AND node for the clause (1). Next the first subgoal is invoked (2) selecting the OR node for the parent procedure. In step (3) the first parent clause is selected and returns the binding "mary" for the variable Z. Note the OR node still has remaining choices. With the first parent subgoal succeeding, the AND node continues to the second and invokes another parent procedure (4). The OR node tries each of the clauses of the parent procedure (5,6,7,8) trying to satisfy the subgoal

parent(X,mary).

---

grandparent(X,Y) :- parent(Z,Y) , parent(X,Z).

parent(mary,tom).
parent(john,tom).
parent(alice,john).
parent(paul,john).

Figure 1.3: A Prolog Example.

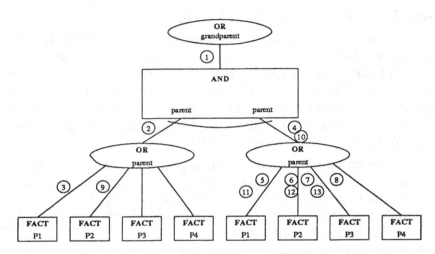

Figure 1.4: Search Tree for grandparent Database

When no clauses remain in this OR node, backtracking returns to the last OR node executed with outstanding choices, namely the OR node for the first parent subgoal. At this point, the variable binding for Z is undone and the next clause of parent is invoked (9). This time parent returns the binding "john" for Z. The grandparent AND node then proceeds forward again (10) to invoke the second parent subgoal as

parent(X,john).

The OR node for this invocation of parent then sequences through the AND nodes for the parent procedure until it finds a clause which satisfies the goal (11,12,13). At this point grandparent succeeds with the binding

$$A = alice.$$

Some Example Applications in Prolog.

The model for Prolog in the previous section shows it to be well suited for problems requiring a solution to be found by a search of the problem space. This is a predominant paradigm of Artificial Intelligence [44]. The fields of natural language processing and knowledge representation have been mentioned previously. Two other classic fields requiring search are games and problem solving. Here the problem is:

> Given an initial state (e.g. board position) and a desired final state or goal (e.g. a winning position) and a collection of rules for transforming from one state to another (e.g. legal moves); find a sequence of transformations which proceed from the initial state to the final state.

In Prolog, such a problem may be posed with the query:

$$?- solve(InitState, FinalState).$$

Solve may be defined as:

```
solve(X,Y) :- rule(X,Y).
solve(X,Y) :- rule(X,T) , solve(T,Y).
```

where the database contains the representation of state transformation rules.

As another example, Despain [16] describes the design of computer architectures in terms of a search tree. Here, design decisions to be made at each level of a design can be represented as alternative clauses in a Prolog procedure for that level, and requirements and mutual constraints can be described by the subgoals within the body of each clause. Additional examples of

Computer Aided Design applications at lower levels can be found in the work of Barrow [5] on digital circuit design and Hill and Roy [29] and Mcgeer etal. [40] on VLSI design and layout.

A related area is that of simulation. A Prolog program describing the design of a system is itself a simulator for the system. Figure 1.5, due to Despain, is a Prolog program describing a very simple processor at the register transfer level. This program, together with an appropriate set of queries (test vectors) may be executed by a Prolog system to simulate and verify the design. A similar project has written a simulator in Prolog of the Prolog Machine (PLM), the processor described later in this book.

Prolog may also be used to do symbolic manipulation of algebraic expressions to simplify or solve them. Figure 1.6, due to Warren [63], is one example of a symbolic differentiation program. The PRESS system is another such system to solve algebraic equations [9].

Another application suggested by Warren in his thesis, is the use of Prolog to write compilers. This suggestion has been put to use by Van Roy [61] to write a Prolog compiler for the PLM in Prolog.

Progress in Prolog Implementations.

At its inception, Prolog, like LISP, was implemented as an interpreted language [51]. The highly interactive nature of the language provided a major impetus in this direction. A great deal of effort has been applied to realizing efficient implementations of such interpreters [23]. A major innovation occurred with the approach put forward by David Warren [63] to compile Prolog for more efficient execution. With a compiler, some of the operations and decisions which must occur dynamically and repeatedly at run time in an interpreter can be made statically and only once at compile time. Compile time operations also include analysis to provide features for more efficient run time performance (e.g.

```
run(AC, PC) :- fetch(PC, P1, OP, X),
          execute(OP, X, AC, A, P1, P),
          run(A, P).
run(halt, _, _).

fetch(PC, P1, OP, X) :-  P1 is PC + 1,  m(PC, OP, X).

execute(add, X, AC, A, PC, PC) :- m(X, T), A is T + AC, !.
execute(and, X, AC, A, PC, PC) :- m(X, T), A is T / AC, !.
execute(load,X, AC, A, PC, PC) :- m(X, A), !.
execute(stor,X, AC, AC,PC, PC) :- m(X, _), !, retract((m(X, _))),
                                  assert((m(X, AC))).
execute(stor,X, AC, AC,PC, PC) :- assert((m(X, AC))), !.
execute(jump,X, AC, AC,PC, X ).
execute(brn ,X, AC, AC,PC, X ) :- AC < 0, !.
execute(brn ,X, AC, AC,PC, PC ).
execute(shr ,X, AC, A, PC, PC) :- A is AC >> 1, !.
execute(comp,X, AC, A, PC, PC) :- A is AC , !.

run :- run(0, 0), m(10, Ans), print(Ans).

m(0,add, 8).       m(1,add, 9).
m(2,stor,10).      m(3,halt,_).
m(8,2).            m(9,3).
```

Figure 1.5: A Simple Machine Simulator

?--   times10(X), d(X,Y), write(Y), nl.
?--   divide10(X), d(X,Y), write(Y), nl.
?--   log10(X),   d(X,Y), write(Y), nl.
?--   ops8(X),   d(X,Y), write(Y), nl.

d(U+V,X,DU+DV) :- !, d(U,X,DU), d(V,X,DV).
d(U-V,X,DU-DV) :- !, d(U,X,DU), d(V,X,DV).
d(U*V,X,DU*V+U*DV) :- !, d(U,X,DU), d(V,X,DV).
d(U/V,X,(DU*V-U*DV)/(^(V,2))) :- !, d(U,X,DU), d(V,X,DV).
d(^(U,N),X,DU*N*(^(U,N1))) :- !, integer(N), is(N1,N,-,1), d(U,X,DU).
d(-U,X,-DU) :- !, d(U,X,DU).
d(exp(U),X,exp(U)*DU) :- !, d(U,X,DU).
d(log(U),X,DU/U) :- !, d(U,X,DU).
d(X,X,1).
d(C,X,0).

times10((((((((((x*x)*x)*x)*x)*x)*x)*x)*x)*x).
divide10((((((((((x/x)/x)/x)/x)/x)/x)/x)/x)/x).
log10(log(log(log(log(log(log(log(log(log(log(x))))))))))).
ops8((x+1)*(^(x,2)+2)*(^(x,3)+3)).

Figure 1.6: Symbolic Differentiation

---

indexing) and memory usage (e.g. generalized tail recursion optimization). Warren's compiler translated Prolog to an intermediate form based on a set of operations fundamental to Prolog which could then be implemented on a target machine, in his case the DEC-10.

The next step in this progression is the design of an architecture to directly execute the compiled intermediate form. An early proposal in this area by Tick and Warren [57] led to our work [21, 22] in the design of a Prolog processor, the PLM.

COMPUTER ARCHITECTURE

Most computers in existence today adhere to the von Neumann model of execution. This was particularly true in the early days of those machines which would be considered computers today. At that time, the size and nature of the problems addressed to these machines and the simple, elegant and efficient von Neumann model led to the concept of the General Purpose Computer. Such a computer was visualized as a single machine capable of efficiently solving any problem posed to it. As the size of the problems grew and the nature of the applications broadened, architects began to realize that in order to maintain and improve efficiency, the designs had to be modified. A first step in this direction was the automation of some of the functions normally carried out in software. An example of this is the inclusion of circuitry for integer multiplication in the processing unit. This trend evolved into specialized coprocessors such as a floating point coprocessor which incorporated separate functional units with their own control to perform very specialized tasks yet remain under the overall command of the Control unit of the machine. Such specialized machines will be called **tightly coupled coprocessors** in this book. Examples include the floating point unit in the IBM 360/91 [59] and floating point accelerator chips such as the 68881 and 80287 coprocessors. Another example of a coprocessor specialized to replace a software function is address translation hardware for implementing virtual addressing in memory. These steps represent minor deviations from the basic von Neumann model.

The next logical step in this progression is independent multi-processors included in a system. This could take the form of several "general purpose" processors or the addition of specialized processors. A prime example of a specialized processor is the I/O channel processors (IOP) of the IBM 360 machines. Here a specialized function, I/O, was separated into an independent processor with its own instruction set and control. I/O operations are initiated by the CPU and are executed in parallel by the IOP running its own program with status reported back to the CPU on completion. This scheme will be referred to as **loosely coupled coprocessors.**

The principle of a loosely coupled coprocessor can also be applied to a specialized language coprocessor to perform language specific operations. The implementation of these language specific operations in specialized hardware directed at the problem being addressed and its software system has precedent in earlier computer systems. Examples include the SYMBOL computer [54], the IBM System/38 [15], and other high level language machines. Such processors may provide either direct execution of a high level language or directly support only critical features of such languages in the architecture. This trend continues today with the advent of the LISP machines [1] and now Prolog machines.

Thus the overall trend has been diverging from the General Purpose Computer toward collections of specialized processors and from the traditional von Neumann machine toward parallelism in function and control. The concept behind this trend is that rather than designing a general purpose processor expected to execute a variety of programming styles each with a different collection of fundamental operations, an architecture should consist of a collection of processors each tuned to be very good at one aspect of the problem at hand. Such is the case of the Prolog Machine described here.

OTHER SYMBOLIC COMPUTING PROCESSORS

Special purpose processor for symbolic computing have been proposed and built in the past. Several examples are described here.

The Japanese PSI.

The PSI is designed to "...establish a good programming environment for logic programming" [45] as a first step in the Fifth Generation Computer project. It is designed to be a stand-alone personal workstation machine and therefore incorporates not only support for logic programming but also support for operating system functions and such features as editors, debuggers and associated user communication operations. The approach taken is to extend Prolog via appropriate built-in functions for these needs.

The Instruction Set Architecture (ISA) of the PSI is built around the KL0 (Kernel Language 0) machine language [11] which is based on an internal direct representation of Prolog programs. KL0 is interpreted by the microcode of the machine. Thus the PSI can be considered to be a direct execution high level architecture.

Some of the features of the PSI architecture include a tagged representation of data to allow hardware support of type checking operations (frequent in symbolic processing), support for virtual addressing for the large memory requirements typical of Prolog applications, and a multi-stack model. The PSI has recently been demonstrated and performs at between 20 and 30 KLIPS [42] (Kilo Logical Inferences Per Second).

A second experiment conducted on the PSI write microcode for the machine to emulate the WAM. The design includes four stacks for global, local and trail data as well as a control stack for environment and backtracking information. Results from this experiment show a factor of 2 performance gain over the microcode interpreter PSI.

The LISP Machines.

Another approach to symbolic processing is the employment of the LISP language, and two examples of specialized processors for LISP are presented.

The first is the Symbolics 3600 which grew out of research at MIT in the mid 70's and is the successor of the Symbolics LM-2 introduced in 1981 [41]. The 3600 is also designed to be a standalone workstation system. However, the design includes the LISP processor as well as several other 68000-based processors (the Front End Processor, FEP, and the Console Processor) for managing communications and other I/O.

The 3600 processor provides support for LISP, not direct execution of LISP. Thus LISP programs are compiled into the 3600 instruction set. The instruction set includes traditional instruction categories such as data movement, calling, branch, and arithmetic instructions as well as specialized list and symbol instructions (e.g. car, cdr, rplaca). The instructions are zero or one address instructions which make use of a stack to store operands. Two large stack buffers are provided to reduce memory bandwidth. Other features of the 3600 include a tagged architecture for hardware type checking, including a cdr-coded list representation, and an intelligent instruction fetch unit which caches up to 2K instructions and performs the instruction decode to obtain a microcode address. In addition, support for virtual addressing is provided with specialized caches to assist address translation via a combination of software, firmware and hardware. The 3600 also provides special hardware assist for an incremental garbage collection system [1], a frequent operation in LISP.

A second LISP processor is the Scheme-79 [56] designed to be a single chip microcomputer LISP machine. The Scheme-79 chooses to represent LISP code directly as lists in memory, called S-code. The S-code is then interpreted by microcode, i.e. this is direct execution architecture. All items in memory are thus represented uniformly as lists; code, data, and even the single stack. Other features of the Scheme-79 include a tagged architecture, hardware support for virtual addressing, and special hardware assistance for heap allocation, a frequent operation since everything is a list.

The SPUR Project.

The SPUR (Symbolic Processing Using RISCs) [30] project at Berkeley is a RISC (Reduced Instruction Set Computer) architecture for general purpose computing with specialized support for symbolic processing, particularly LISP. SPUR is an extension of earlier Berkeley RISC architectures RISC I, RISC II, and SOAR [32, 47, 60]. The primary extensions include the tag support for LISP and associated instruction set enhancements and a tightly coupled coprocessor interface intended for a Floating Point coprocessor. To support general purpose computing, and in particular, an operating system, the SPUR processor is capable of handling traps and interrupts. As a result all SPUR instructions must be restartable.

Tag support in SPUR takes the form of specialized instructions for comparing and branching on tags and for loading and storing tagged data. Tagged data in SPUR is represented in 40 bit words, 8 bits for the tags and 32 bits for data. In memory tagged data is stored in two 32 bit words thus requiring two memory references for each tagged access. However, the SPUR cache and internal data paths support the 40 bit format.

A study has been conducted using the SPUR simulator for running Prolog on SPUR [7]. The implementation chosen was a macro expansion of the PLM code for Prolog (presented in this book) into SPUR code. Over a collection of benchmark programs for the PLM discussed in Dobry etal. [22] the static code size in bytes of the SPUR code was from 16.90 to 51.08 times that for the PLM with an average of 26.11. Dynamically, SPUR executed from 1.96 to 4.09 times the number of cycles as the PLM with an average of 2.31.

The work also suggested adding a microcoded coprocessor to SPUR with an architecture which is a "hybrid of the PLM and SPUR architectures." Preliminary estimates on SPUR with this coprocessor show performance comparable to the PLM.

MOTIVATION

An earlier section concluded stating that the trend is away from the General Purpose Processors. Instead one should realize we are evolving toward General Purpose Computing Systems composed of multiple, special-purpose processors. The primary motivating hypotheses behind the work described here are that:

(1)   To achieve high performance, a computer architecture should be composed of a collection of elements each of which is specialized in a particular problem or class of problems.

(2)   A specialized processor should be designed with an instruction set and architecture to provide *support* for the target problem rather than for direct execution of a high level language as in the original PSI microcode.

(3)   Specialization and parallelism should be manifest at all levels of the design including specialized hardware functional units at the level of the microarchitecture.

In particular, the research discussed here is to investigate the application of these principles to the design of a specialized processor architecture for Prolog programs. Table 1.1 taken from Warren [63], shows that a twenty fold increase in performance can be achieved for Prolog with a compiler based implementation. The Table also shows the ideal simulated performance for the PLM.

Based on these results, the intent of this book is to show that:

An additional ten fold improvement in performance can be realized for sequential execution of Prolog programs over implementations on general purpose processors by a processor specifically designed and tuned to the Prolog task.

In support of this theme, the following problems are addressed.

(1)   Unification is a fundamental operation of Prolog so efficient unification must be supported by the processor.

Benchmark	Execution Time (msec)		
	Prolog-10I Interpreter	Prolog-10 Compiler	PLM Machine
nrev1	1160	53.7	2.15
qs4	1344	75.0	4.44
serialize			
palin25	602	40.2	2.45
differen			
times10	76.2	3.00	
divide10	84.4	2.94	
log10	49.2	1.92	
ops8	63.7	2.24	
	273.5	10.1	0.77
query	8888	185	17.13

Table 1.1: Comparison with Warren Results

(2)   Backtracking is a fundamental operation of Prolog so an efficient means of saving and restoring the state of a logic program must be provided. This state takes two forms: the structure of the search tree above the point at which an alternate clause is selected, and the binding status of variables at these tree branch points.

(3)   Numeric and other non-logic operations are required to support general computations. An effective *escape* mechanism must be provided to direct these operations to an appropriate processor with an efficient means of passing arguments and results.

(4)   Symbolic data is the mainstay of a Prolog program. An efficient means of representing and manipulating this data

must be provided.

(5)   Memory bandwidth is a particularly acute problem in Prolog execution. A cost effective means of realizing sufficient bandwidth must be provided.

CONTRIBUTIONS

The major contributions presented in this book are:

(1)   A complete ISA description of a processor for Prolog in the form of extensions and enhancements to the Abstract Prolog Machine proposed by Warren [64].

(2)   Extensions to include implementation of the cut operation of Prolog and an efficient escape mechanism for implementing Prolog built-ins.

(3)   Enhancements to include a refinement of mechanisms for indexing Prolog clauses and an alternative backtracking scheme to reduce backtracking overhead.

(4)   Mechanisms to implement assert and retract for compiled Prolog code.

(5)   A microarchitecture specification for implementing the proposed ISA.

(6)   Buffering and caching schemes to deal with memory bandwidth restrictions.

(7)   An analysis of the effects of these various features on performance.

(8)   A physical implementation of the PLM in TTL which runs with a 10MHz clock.

ORGANIZATION

Chapter 1 has provided the motivation for symbolic computing and specifically Logic Programming and describes the Prolog language. Several related architectures for symbolic processing were also described. Chapter 2 gives a description of an abstract machine for Prolog based on the work of Warren. In Chapter 3 the abstract machine description is filled in to specify the proposed architecture of the PLM. Chapter 4 describes the design considerations for implementing the architecture in hardware. Chapter 5 describes the results of simulations studies of the architecture and suggests improvements at all levels of the design. Finally, Chapter 6 draws conclusions on what was learned and suggests further enhancements and alternatives in the design to improve performance.

CHAPTER 2

AN ABSTRACT PROLOG MACHINE

THE WAM

In 1977 David Warren described an instruction set and execution model for compiled Prolog [63]. This design was later modified and provided as an abstract machine specification which has become know as the Warren Abstract Machine (WAM) [57, 64]. The architecture described in this book extends the WAM and provides a description of the resulting machine and its implementation in hardware.

This Chapter describes the WAM, its data types, memory configuration and instruction set. Modifications and enhancements to the WAM are described in the next Chapter laying the groundwork for implementation of an architecture for Prolog described and analyzed in subsequent chapters.

DATA TYPES

The WAM specification calls for a tagged architecture with tags used to identify the data type of each data item. There are four data types in Prolog. These four types are reflected in the WAM data representation as follows:

REFERENCE data items are used to represent Prolog variables. A variable may be either unbound or bound to the value of another data item in the Data Space. A bound Reference data item contains a pointer to its value. A common convention for unbound variables is to have them point to themselves.

CONSTANT data items represent various constants in Prolog, e.g. atoms, integers, etc. The instruction set treats all constants in the same manner regardless of what they represent (with the single exception of the constant NIL). However, the programmer has a collection of built-in functions available which can distinguish and operate on constants based on their meaning.

COMPOUND data items represent compound terms of Prolog. This classification consists primarily of a data type called a *structure* which consists of a functor (an atom), an arity, **n**, and n elements, each of which may be any Prolog item. For example, the structure

$$f/3(a, b, c)$$

is a compound term with functor "f", arity 3, and three elements; "a","b", and "c". In the WAM structures are represented by a memory location tagged as a structure containing a pointer to a contiguous block of memory holding the functor followed by the

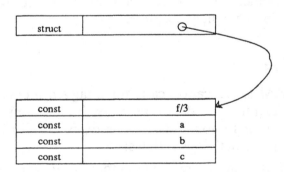

Figure 2.1: Structure Representation

elements as seen in Figure 2.1.

A second type of compound term available in Prolog is the *list*. As in LISP, a list is a linked collection of elements each one containing an arbitrary term and a pointer to the next element terminated by the special atom NIL. Each such element is referred to as a "dotted pair" [38]. For example, the list represented in Prolog syntax by

$$[a, b, c]$$

consists of three dotted pairs. Borrowing LISP syntax, this can be explicitly represented using the infix operator "." as follows:

$$(a . (b . (c . NIL)))$$

That is, the element with term "a" (called the **car**) and a pointer (called the **cdr**) to an element with car "b" and cdr pointing to an element with car "c" and cdr, the terminating atom NIL. A straightforward mapping to Prolog is to represent each element of a list as a structure with functor "." of arity 2 whose elements are the car and cdr. The example above is shown in Figure 2.2a. In the WAM a more efficient representation is used by substituting a list tag for the structure pointer and ./2 functor as shown in Figure 2.2b. This representation is more efficient in space (no functor need be stored) and time (no functor need be processed).

MEMORY AREAS

The memory space of the WAM is divided into two distinct areas, the Code Space and the Data Space. The Code Space contains the WAM instructions which constitute programs, procedures, and clauses. The Data Space is where Prolog data and computation state are stored and is the area of memory where all data reading and writing take place. It is further divided into three major areas, the Stack, the Heap, and the Trail. In addition a

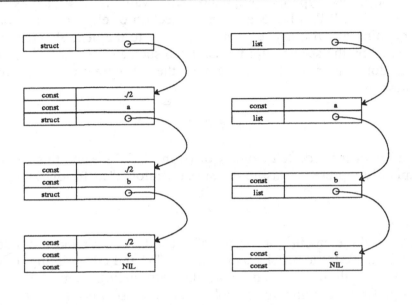

a   b

Figure 2.2: List Representation

scratch area called the PDL (Push Down List) is provided for use during unification. The WAM specification also includes processor registers which point into the memory areas as well as hold data values in the processor. Some of the terms introduced in this section are only briefly explained, but are clarified in the subsequent section dealing with the instruction set.

Figure 2.3 shows the Code Space which holds the instructions representing Prolog procedures and clauses. Two registers point into the Code space. The P register or Program Pointer is the register which contains the address of the next instruction to be

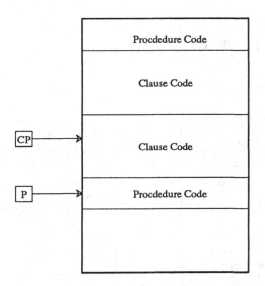

Figure 2.3: Code Space Organization

executed. This is the program counter of a conventional processor. The CP register or Continuation Pointer contains the address of the next instruction to be executed upon successful completion of the current clause. This is analogous to a return pointer.

Figure 2.4 shows the Data Space with its major areas and the registers pointing into each. The Heap is the area of the Data Space used for storage of compound terms, i.e. lists and structures, as well as globalized unsafe variables (to be explained in later sections). The Heap is allocated as a LIFO and in general only deallocated upon backtracking. Heap entries may also be reclaimed by garbage collection. The top of the Heap is indicated by the H or Heap Pointer register. An additional register, the HB or Heap

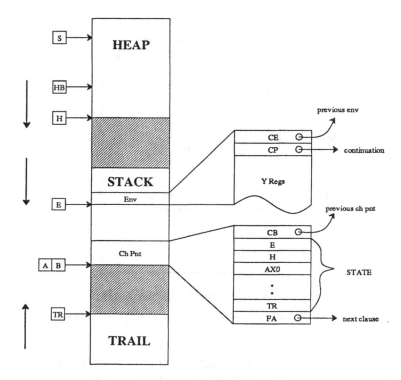

Figure 2.4: Data Space Configuration

Backtrack Pointer contains a pointer to the top of the Heap at the last backtracking point (choice point). It is used to reclaim Heap space upon backtracking and to make trailing decisions. Finally an S register or Structure Pointer is provided to indicate the next element of a compound term during list or structure processing.

The Stack is the primary working area in the Data Space. Space is allocated and deallocated as a LIFO in blocks or frames of two possible classes; **environment frames** and **choice point frames.**

An environment frame is a variable sized frame allocated for a clause which contains some state information and space for an arbitrary number of permanent variables used in the environment. The state information includes a *CE* entry containing a pointer to the previous environment frame (thus all environment frames are linked throughout the Stack) and a *CP* entry containing the value of the CP register when the environment was activated. This entry is used to restore CP when a previous environment is reactivated. Some variables are also stored in the environment and are referred to as permanent variables or Y registers. The current environment is indicated by the E register or Environment Pointer.

A choice point frame is a fixed sized block containing a snapshot of the processor state to be restored upon backtracking. The entries include a *CB* entry pointing to the previous choice point frame (thus linking all choice points on the Stack), a *FA* entry (Failure Address) containing a Code Space address of the instruction to be executed when failure occurs, and other entries which define the state of the computation to be restored on backtracking. The B register or Backtrack Pointer points to the current choice point.

The WAM specification provides for a Top of Stack register, A. As will be seen in the next section, either a choice point or an environment may be at the top of the Stack.

The Trail is the area of the Data Space used to keep track of variable bindings which must be unbound upon backtracking. It is maintained as a LIFO whose top is indicated by the TR register. Entries on the Trail consist of pointers to variables. They are inserted when variables are bound and deleted during backtracking.

Finally, the PDL (not shown) is a scratch pad area of the Data Space used during unification of two compound terms. Entries on the PDL consist of pairs of pointers to positions in the two terms as

unification proceeds. Such entries are pushed onto the PDL when
the unification operation must be used recursively as with nested
lists or structures. The unification of two such terms is complete
only when the PDL is empty.

The remaining processor registers are the AX registers. They
are used to pass parameters during procedure invocation as well as
to hold temporary variables. The number of AX registers is not
specified by the WAM.

SOME DEFINITIONS

Before describing the instructions themselves, a few terms
are defined.

In the WAM, variables may be classified as either **permanent** or **temporary** with temporary variables stored in available AX registers and permanent variables stored in the environment. Variables are stored in temporaries whenever possible
unless the register contents could be destroyed before it is used.
Subgoal invocation is one thing that could destroy the contents of
AX registers as subgoals have free reign to use the registers as
necessary. Variables which must survive across procedure calls
are called permanent and are stored in the environment on the
Stack. Temporary variables for which there are no available AX
registers may also be stored in the environment.

For example, in the grandparent procedure described in
Chapter 1, the clause

grandparent(X , Y) :- parent(X , Z), parent(Z , Y).

the variable X is only used in the first subgoal, therefore its value
may remain in an AX register. However, the value of the variable
Y must be preserved to be used for the second subgoal. Since the
parent procedure (and its descendants) can arbitrarily change the
values in AX registers, Y cannot reliably remain in a temporary

and must be stored in the environment. Likewise with Z, even though Z is created in the grandparent clause (i.e. Z is called a local variable) it is not guaranteed that the value will remain in a register when the first subgoal returns. Therefore Z is also stored in the environment.

A second term used below is **unification mode.** Unification may be performed in either of two ways; as a pattern matcher, termed read mode, or as a term constructor, termed write mode. The distinction is made dynamically (at run time) in Prolog so the instructions of the WAM must also make the decision as they are executed. Using the grandparent example again, assume grandparent is invoked with the query

$$?- grandparent(A, B).$$

which asks for all pairs, A and B, for whom the relation holds. The first subgoal is then invoked as

$$parent(A, Z).$$

asking for any pair, A and Z, for whom parent holds. The parent procedure, a collection of facts, will bind A and Z; i.e. unification takes place in write mode constructing bindings for the variables, say

$$A = mary$$
$$Z = tom$$

The second subgoal is then invoked as

$$parent(mary, B)$$

with B remaining unbound. The same code for the parent procedure must now match "mary" to values in the clause heads; i.e. execution of instructions for unifying the first argument proceeds in read mode. In most instructions the mode of unification need be remembered only within the execution of the instruction. However, for unifying compound terms, a sequence of instructions may be used. Therefore the unification mode must be preserved across instruction boundaries. This is done in the WAM with a mode bit stating whether unification is to proceed in read or write mode.

INSTRUCTION SET

This section describes the WAM instruction set. Modifications made for the PLM are described in the next Chapter. The WAM instruction set implements the AND/OR search tree of a Prolog program. The OR nodes of the tree contain what will be called **procedure code** and the AND nodes contain **clause code**. The complete instruction set may be divided into six classes; three for control and three for data manipulation. The classes are:

Procedure Control
Indexing
Clause Control
Get
Put
Unify

Each class of instructions will be discussed in turn describing their effects on the state of the machine.

Procedure Code.

The procedure control instructions implement the OR nodes of the search tree as seen in Figure 2.5. They come in pairs:

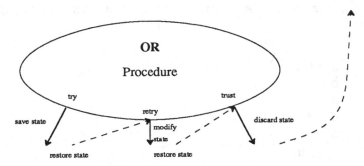

Figure 2.5: An OR Node

try_me_else	L	try	L
retry_me_else	L	retry	L
trust_me_else	fail	trust	L

The "try" pair create a new choice point at the top of the Stack. A try instruction occurs before the execution of clause code for the first clause to be attempted in a procedure. The action of these instructions is to place a choice point at the top of the Stack which includes the current B register value, thus linking all choice points on the Stack, and the H register indicating the current top of the Heap. Any data added to the Heap after a try instruction would no longer be required should failure occur with this choice point current. Thus the H register in the choice point allows a portion of the Heap to be reclaimed on backtracking. The choice point also contains the current value of the TR register. Variable bindings added to the Trail after the choice point is created are those that must be unbound on backtracking. The remainder of the processor state in the form of register values is also placed in the choice point to be restored on backtracking. It should be noted that the position of the choice point on the Stack carries implicit state information. All environments earlier on the Stack will become active on backtracking even if they had been deactivated during forward execution. As further explanation, for the Prolog program:

```
a :- b,e.
b :- c.
c.
c :- d.
d.
e :- fail.
```

when the choice point is created for the procedure "c", environments will have been created for the clauses of procedures "a" and "b" and the Stack will appear as shown in Figure 2.6a. The environment for "b" is the current environment while those for both "a" and "b" are active. When procedure "c" succeeds, and thus procedure "b" succeeds, the environment for "b" is no longer required for forward execution and is therefore deactivated. Figure 2.6b shows the Stack just prior to invoking "e" as a subgoal in procedure "a". Note that the current and only active environment on the Stack is that for "a" but that the space for the environment for "b" has not been reclaimed. When "e" fails, the state of the machine, including the Stack, must be restored as it was at the invocation of "c", namely that in Figure 2.6a. The position of the choice point on the Stack accomplishes this function. Thus it can be observed that Stack space is not reclaimed before the current choice point.

The final entry placed in the choice point by the try instruction is the failure address. This indicates where execution should continue should failure occur. The value placed in the failure address is determined by the form of the try instruction used. With the **try_me_else** instruction, the failure address is the operand L.

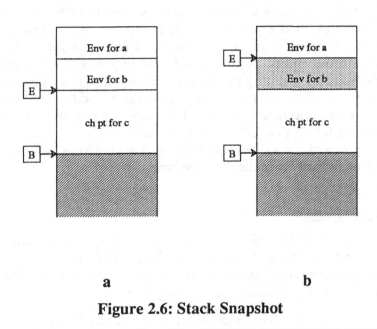

a   b

Figure 2.6: Stack Snapshot

In forward execution the clause code for the first clause to be tried immediately follows the **try_me_else** instruction. With the **try** instruction the failure address points to the instruction immediately following and the clause code for the first clause to be tried is indicated by the operand L. The instruction at the failure address will always be another procedure control instruction. The last action of the try instruction is to update the B register to make the newly created choice point current.

The solid arrow in Figure 2.5 shows the forward execution path from the OR node once the choice point has been created. Should backtracking occur to this OR node, as indicated by the dashed arrow, control returns to the procedure control instruction at the failure address after the state has been restored from the choice point.

If there are more than two branches from the OR node subsequent clauses in the procedure begin with a "retry" instruction. Since the state to be restored on the next failure is the same as is already in the choice point, the retry simply modifies the current choice point by updating the failure address. The retry instructions also have two forms for determining the failure address as with the try. The last branch from the OR node begins with a "trust" instruction which discards the current choice point by restoring the B and HB register values. Subsequent backtracking will occur to an OR node further up the decision tree.

Indexing Code.

A second class of instructions used to generate procedure code are the indexing instructions. These act as filters to prevent attempts to execute clauses which the compiler can determine will not unify with the invoking goal. They are:

$$
\begin{array}{ll}
\text{switch\_on\_term} & \text{Lv,Lc,Ll,Ls} \\
\text{switch\_on\_constant} & \text{T,N} \\
\text{switch\_on\_structure} & \text{T,N}
\end{array}
$$

The **switch_on_term** instruction branches based on the type of the first argument of the invoking goal to either Lv, Lc, Ll, or Ls for a variable, constant, list, or structure respectively. This filtering on type identifies four blocks of procedure code. For the constant and structure block further filtering is possible. The **switch_on_constant** (**switch_on_structure**) instruction filters clauses by hashing on the value of the constant (functor of the structure) in the first argument and entering a hash table of size N at address T to find the branch address. The code blocks selected by the filtering instructions include the necessary procedure control instructions to sequence through the appropriate clauses. A generic procedure code sequence is shown in Figure 2.7. Clauses are first filtered by the **switch_on_term** instruction based on the type of the first argument with which the procedure is invoked. This identifies four blocks of procedure code; the variable block, constant block, list block and structure block. Within each block the Prolog order for clauses of top to bottom is realized

	switch_on_term	Lc,Ll,Ls
	try_me_else	V1
	clause code	1
V1:	retry_me_else	V2
V1a:	clause code	2
	...	
Vn-1:	trust_me_else	fail
Vn-1a:	clause code	n
Lc:	CONSTANT	BLOCK
Ll:	try	Vk1a
	retry	Vk2a
	...	
	trust	Vkja
Ls:	STRUCTURE	BLOCK

Figure 2.7: Typical Procedure Code

by the order the clause blocks are sequenced by procedure control instructions.

A procedure called with a variable in the first argument will unify with any data item in the first parameter. The variable block uses the "_me_else" versions of the procedure control instructions to link all of the clause blocks. A procedure called with a list in the first argument need try only those clauses with either a list or variable first parameter. The list block consists of a sequence of a single try, zero or more retry and a single trust instruction pointing to the appropriate blocks of clause code. (It should be noted that if any procedure block has only a single clause then choice point instructions are not needed and the clause block can be indicated in the **switch_on_term** instruction. Likewise if any procedure block has no clauses, a fail may be indicated in the **switch_on_term**).

The constant and structure blocks are similar in form. For these blocks all clauses with either a constant (structure) or variable first parameter form the ordered set of clauses which must be tried. However further filtering of clauses can be done using the **switch_on_constant** (**switch_on_structure**) instruction creating subsets of clauses which can be identified by the value of the constant (functor of the structure) in the invoking argument. The Constant and Structure Blocks shown in the Figure will be discussed in detail in Chapter 3.

An OR node with indexing instructions is shown in Figure 2.8. The filtering instructions dynamically identify a single block of procedure control instructions for a given invocation of a procedure; i.e. only one such block will be executed for a given invocation of the procedure. The sequencing of clauses (AND nodes) for a complete traversal of each block is shown in the Figure with both forward execution paths (solid lines) and backward execution paths (dashed lines) numbered in sequence.

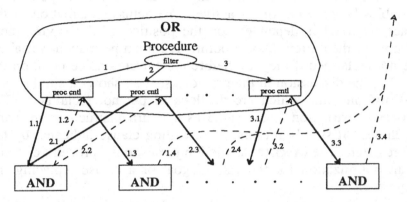

Figure 2.8: OR Node with Indexing Instructions

Clause Code.

The remaining instructions implement the AND nodes of the tree and are therefore used to construct the clause code blocks. These blocks perform data manipulation (described in the next section) and control the sequencing of subgoals with clause control instructions. Clause control instructions are divided into two groups: those for sequencing between subgoals, and those for managing the environment. The instructions for sequencing between subgoals are:

$$\begin{array}{ll} \text{call} & \text{P,N} \\ \text{proceed} & \\ \text{execute} & \text{P} \end{array}$$

The **call** instruction invokes the subgoal procedure P, and states that the size of the environment of the *calling* clause is N. It establishes the return pointer in the CP register. The size argument allows a clause to trim its own environment as processing proceeds from left to right through the subgoals and thus some permanent variables become no longer active. The actual reclamation of the space trimmed is dependent on the position of the environment relative to the current choice point. Trimmed permanent variables are not reclaimed if they are before the current choice point on the Stack. The discussion in the previous section shows a similar case for environments which are deallocated but not reclaimed. The **proceed** instruction is the same as a return instruction on many machines. It simply returns to the calling clause indicated by the CP register. The **execute** instruction jumps to the procedure P, and is an optimization for the last subgoal of a clause replacing the sequence:

> call   P,0
> proceed

This is shown in Figure 2.9. Here the solid arrows represent the subgoal invocation and the dashed arrows the subsequent return. In Figure 2.9a the last subgoal is called and when it returns the clause implemented by the AND node simply returns. Figure 2.9b shows this extra return step eliminated by jumping to the last subgoal with an **execute** so that when it proceeds, control returns to an AND node further up the tree. This is a generalization of the Tail Recursion Optimization and is called the Last Call Optimization.

The control instructions for managing the environment are:

> allocate
> deallocate

The **allocate** instruction establishes a new environment at the top of the Stack, updating the E register to make it current. An environment consists of the permanent variables not yet trimmed, and the state information described previously. The **deallocate**

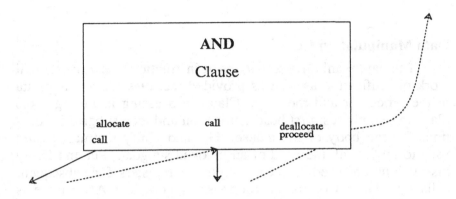

a. Non-optimized Clause Code

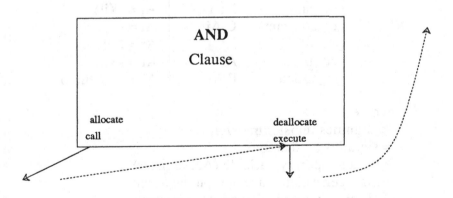

b. Optimized Clause Code

Figure 2.9: Last Call Optimization

instruction removes the current environment from the Stack by restoring the E, and CP registers. This operation deactivates but may not reclaim the environment from the Stack.

Data Manipulation Code.

The data manipulation classes of instructions perform the real work of unification as well as provided facilities for moving data in the processor and memory. Clause processing in Prolog takes place in two phases; first head unification and then subgoal invocations for the body of the clause. Get and Unify instructions are used to unify with the head of an invoked subgoal. Put and Unify instructions are used to set up argument registers for subsequent calls by Clause Control instructions. A complete AND node is shown in Figure 2.10. The Get instructions and their actions are shown below.

get_variable	XilYi,Aj	Aj -> XilYi
get_value	XilYi,Aj	Aj = XilYi
get_constant	C,Ai	Ai = C
get_nil	Ai	Ai = NIL
get_list	Ai	Ai = list
get_structure	F,Ai	Ai = structure F

where
-> signifies register transfer,
= signifies unifications,
Xi is a temporary variable (AX register),
Yi is a permanent variable (on the Stack),
Ai is an argument (also an AX register),
C is a constant,
and F is a functor.

The **get_variable** instruction transfers the contents of Aj to XilYi. It is used the first time a variable appears in the head of the clause

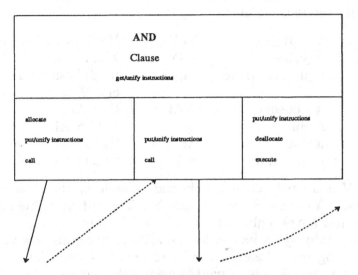

Figure 2.10: A Complete AND Node

and initializes the variable for this environment. Subsequent processing of an initialized variable uses the **get_value** instruction
which unifies the contents of XilYi and Aj. The **get_constant**
instruction unifies the literal constant C with Ai. **Get_nil** is an
optimization of "get_constant NIL." The **get_list** and
get_structure instructions begin the unification of a list or structure with the contents of Ai. Since the unification of such a compound term in the head is compiled into a sequence of instructions
(get followed by unify's) the unification mode and a pointer to the
next element of the term (for read mode) are saved across the
instruction boundaries. In the WAM this is done with a processor
mode bit and the S register. **Get_structure** also unifies the first
element of the term, the functor, with F.

Put instructions are data transfer instructions used to set up the argument registers prior to invoking a subgoal. They do no unification, otherwise they are analogous to the get instructions. These instructions include:

put_variable	Xi|Yi,Aj	V -> Xi|Yi; V -> Aj
put_value	Xi|Yi,Aj	Xi|Yi -> Aj
put_unsafe_value	Yi,Aj	if(Yi is safe) Yi -> Aj
		else V -> Aj
put_constant	C,Ai	C -> Ai
put_nil	Ai	NIL -> Ai
put_list	Ai	list -> Ai
put_structure	F,Ai	structure F -> Ai

where V is a newly created unbound variable on the Heap (for X and unsafe Y) or the Stack (for safe Y). The **put_variable** instruction creates a new unbound variable in Xi|Yi and puts a reference pointer to it in Aj. Note that for the X case, since this new variable is not being immediately bound and unbound variables may not reside in a register, **put_variable** creates the variable at the top of the Heap. **Put_value** copies the value of Xi|Yi to Aj. **Put_unsafe_value** is similar except in the case where the variable in Yi is still unbound and resident in the current environment. In this case the compiler has identified Yi as an unsafe variable, i.e. a permanent variable about to be trimmed by the next call or deallocate. To prevent a dangling pointer, **put_unsafe_value** moves the variable to the top of the Heap and updates the pointer in Aj. This operation is referred to as gloabalizing an unsafe variable. **Put_constant** and **put_nil** place the literal constants in Ai. The **put_list** and **put_structure** instructions begin construction of a compound term. The processor mode bit is set to write by these instructions and they are followed by a sequence of unify instructions.

The unify instructions are used for the construction and unification of compound terms. Such a process begins with the appropriate get or put instructions (**get_list** , **get_structure** or **put_list** , **put_structure**) followed by a series of unify instructions to process each element of the term. The unify instructions behave differently in read and write mode. They are:

		read mode
unify_variable	Xi|Y	next element -> Xi|Yi
unify_value	Xi|Yi	next element = Xi|Yi
unify_local_value	Yi	next element = Yi
unify_constant	Ci	next element = C
unify_nil		next element = NIL
		write mode
unify_variable	Xi|Y	V -> next element; V -> Xi|Yi
unify_value	Xi|Yi	Xi|Yi -> next element
unify_local_value	Yi	if(Yi is safe) Yi -> next elt
		else V -> next element
unify_constant	Ci	C -> next element
unify_nil		NIL -> next element

The operation performed is determined by the mode set by the preceding get or put instruction. Each instruction operates on the next element of the term being processed. The H and S registers are used as pointers into the compound term being constructed (written) or matched (read) respectively. A brief description of each instruction follows.

unify_variable Xi\|Yi -

> Like **get_variable** and **put_variable**, this instruction is used when the next element is a variable which has not occurred previously in the current clause. In read mode, the next item pointed to by the S register (if it exists) is placed in the X\|Y register. If there is no next item, the instruction fails. In write mode, an unbound variable is placed as the next element at the top of the Heap as indicated by the H register. A pointer

reference to this item is placed in the X|Y register.

unify_value Xi|Yi -

>   This instruction is used when the next element is a
>   variable which has occurred previously in the current
>   clause. In read mode, The next item (if it exists)
>   pointed to by the S register is dereferenced and unified
>   with the dereferenced value of the X|Y register. If no
>   next item exists, the instruction fails. In write mode,
>   the dereferenced X|Y register value is placed as the
>   next element as indicated by the H register.

unify_local_value Yi -

>   This instruction is analogous to the **put_unsafe_value**
>   instruction. It is used when the next element is an
>   unsafe variable (a permanent variable residing in the
>   current environment) occurring for the last time in the
>   current clause. In read mode, this instruction behaves
>   like **unify_value**. In write mode, if the dereferenced
>   value of the X|Y register is an unbound variable resid-
>   ing in an environment later on the Stack than the
>   current choice point, a new unbound variable is placed
>   on the Heap as the next element as indicated by the H
>   register, and a pointer reference is placed in the X|Y
>   register. Otherwise, this instruction behaves like
>   **unify_value**.

unify_constant C -

>   This instruction is used when the next element is a
>   Constant item. In read mode, the next item (if it
>   exists) indicated by the S register is dereferenced and
>   unified with the constant, C. If no next item exists, the
>   instruction fails. In write mode, the constant, C, is
>   placed as the next element as indicated by the H regis-
>   ter.

unify_nil -   This instruction is used to terminate processing of a
>   fixed sized list. In read mode, the place of the next

element is checked to verify it contains NIL, if not the instruction fails. In write mode, NIL is placed in the compound term being constructed.

An Example of Compiled Code.

As an example of how Prolog programs are compiled to the instruction set of the WAM, the Prolog program in Figure 2.11

```
grandparent(GP,GC) :-
        parent(P,GC), parent(GP,P).

parent(mary, tom).
parent(john, tom).
parent(alice,john).
parent(paul,john).
```

Figure 2.11: Prolog Code for grandparent

---

is shown compiled in Figure 2.12.

```
procedure grandparent/2
_458:     allocate                        %  grandparent(
          get_variable       Y2,X1        %   GP,GC) :-
          put_variable       Y1,X1
          call       parent/2,2           %  parent(P,GC),
          put_unsafe_value   Y2,X1
          put_unsafe_value   Y1,X2
          deallocate
          execute    parent/2   %  parent(GP,P).


procedure  parent/2
          switch_on_term     _724,fail,fail
_725:     try_me_else        _726
_727:     get_constant       mary,X1 %  parent( mary,
          get_constant       tom,X2  %   tom
          proceed                    %  ).
_726:     retry_me_else      _728
_729:     get_constant       john,X1 %  parent( john,
          get_constant       tom,X2  %   tom
          proceed                    %  ).
_728:     retry_me_else      _730
_731:     get_constant       alice,X1 %  parent( alice,
_730:     trust_me_else      fail
_732:     get_constant       paul,X1 %  parent( paul,
          get_constant       john,X2 %   john
          proceed                    %  ).
_724:     switch_on_constant3,_733
          % Hash Table
_733:     paul       _732
          alice      _731
          john       _729
          mary       _727
```

Figure 2.12: Compiled Code for grandparent

FUNDAMENTAL OPERATIONS

In addition to the instruction set described in the previous section, there are a few fundamental operations which must be provided by the WAM. These include the backtracking operation invoked by failure, binding of variables, trailing of variable bindings, dereferencing of variables, and general unification of terms. These operations have been defined by Warren and are described in more detail in this section.

Failure.

The first of these operations is *fail*. It is invoked should failure occur during unification or by the **fail** instruction and implements backtracking in Prolog. The fail operation takes the following three steps:

fail Step 1:
> *Restore processor registers from the current choice point. If no current choice point, return goal failure.*

fail Step 2:
> *Pop entries from the Trail and change the indicated location to an unbound variable until the top of the Trail is as indicated in the current choice point.*

fail Step 3:
> *Begin execution of instructions at the Code Space Address indicated in the current choice point failure address.*

The actions of Step 1 will, as a side effect, reclaim Heap space and Stack space allocated since the choice point was created by restoring the H and E registers. In Step 2, variables which were bound in forward execution and trailed (trailing decisions are described below) are "detrailed" i.e. the bindings are undone. Finally, Step 3 completes the backward execution step by branching to the failure address.

Variable Binding and Dereferencing.

Prolog variables are represented in the WAM as Reference type data items containing a pointer to their binding or to themselves if they are unbound. As an optimization, when a variable is instantiated (i.e. bound to a non-variable data item) the binding may overwrite the Reference tagged item. This defines the simplest binding rule:

Binding Rule 0:
> *When binding a variable to a nonvariable, overwrite the variable with the binding.*

However, when a variable is bound to another variable, the result is a Reference data item pointing to another Reference data item. In Prolog when a variable is instantiated, all variables bound to it also become instantiated to the value. For example, in the following code:

a:- b(X), d(X).

b(Y) :- c(Y), e(Y).

c(m).
d(m).
e(m).

during head unification when procedure "b" is invoked, the variable X, which is local to procedure "a" is bound to the variable Y local to procedure "b". When "c" is invoked Y becomes instantiated to the atom, **m**. This binding must be reflected in the value of X when "d" is invoked as the second subgoal in procedure "a". To implement the semantics of Prolog variable binding in the WAM, a binding protocol is provided for binding variables to variables.

In the above example, when X and Y are bound there are two possible ways to realize the binding; make Y point to X (bind Y to X) or make X point to Y (bind X to Y). In the later case, shown in Figure 2.13a, when Y is bound to **m** in procedure "c", the Reference data item at Y is overwritten with the Constant data item, **m** (Figure 2.13b). Since X points to the location of Y, X appears to take the value **m** also. However, when "b" returns to procedure "a" its environment is no longer needed and has been deallocated (deactivated and possibly reclaimed). In this case, X is pointing to a non-allocated variable and its value is potentially lost (Figure 2.13c). The correct binding strategy is to bind Y to X (Figure 2.13d). Now when Y is bound to **m**, the Constant is place at the location of X (Figure 2.13e). Now when "b" deallocates its environment and returns, X retains its binding (Figure 2.13f).

The above observations allow us to define the following binding rule:

Binding Rule 1:
>   *When binding a variable to a variable the younger variable should point to the older variable, i.e. variable pointers should always point to earlier locations on the Stack.*

A second rule is immediately obvious from the previous discussion:

Binding Rule 2:
>   *When binding a variable, the binding should take place at the end of any reference chain beginning at the variable, i.e. bindings should take place at the fully dereferenced value of a variable.*

Corollary:
>   *The binding (value) of a variable is found at the end of the reference chain.*

Rule 2 provides for the operation of dereferencing. Dereferencing is defined as follows:

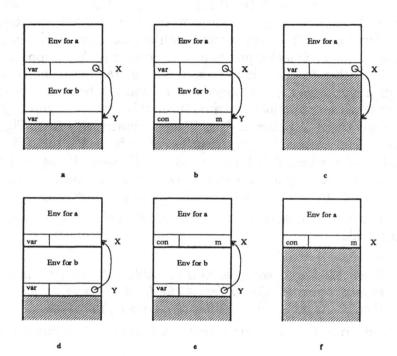

Figure 2.13: Variable Binding Strategies

DEFINITION:

Rule 1: If V contains a non-variable, dereference(V) is the value at V.

Rule 2: else if V contains an unbound variable (a Reference to V), dereference(V) is the value at V.

Rule 3: else V contains a reference to U (U != V),
dereference(V) is dereference(U).

Note the definition is recursive. In the previous example the length of the reference chain was 1, however it is possible to bind variables to obtain arbitrary length reference chains. For example, for the code:

a :- b(X).

b(Y) :- c(A,B), B = Y, d(A).

c(Z,Z).

d(m).

where = is the unify operator of Prolog, Figure 2.14 shows the Stack just prior to invoking procedure "d". During head unification in procedure "b", Y was bound to X. Procedure "c" then bound A to B. Finally the unify operator bound B to the dereferenced value of Y. In order to bind A to **m** in procedure "d", the dereference operation must follow a chain of length 2.

One additional Binding Rule is needed, namely for the case of binding a variable on the Stack and a variable on the Heap. Two possibilities exist, bind Heap to Stack or bind Stack to Heap. Consider the first case for the code:

```
f        :- a(Z), g(Z).
a(Y)     :- b(X, Y), c(X, Y).
b(A, B)        :- d(A, B).
c(_,_).
d(W, [W]).
```

Figure 2.15 traces the generation of the Stack for this example. Figure 2.15a shows the environment for "f" with local variable Z just prior to invoking subgoal "a". In Figure 2.15b the head

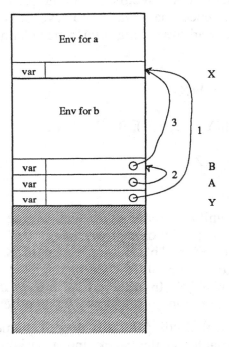

Figure 2.14: A Reference Chain of length 2

unification in procedure "a" has completed binding the local variable Y in "a" to the variable Z in "f" by Binding Rule 1. Figure 2.15b also shows the creation of the local variable X in the environment for "a". After head unification for procedure "b" (Figure 2.15c) the local variable A is bound to X in "a" and B is bound to the fully dereferenced value of Y, namely Z in the environment for "f" (Binding Rule 2). When "d" is invoked a list is created on the Heap bound to Z with a variable bound to the fully dereferenced value of A, namely X in the environment of "a" (Figure 2.15d). No binding rule violations have occurred to this point and all variables have been safe. When "a" returns to "f",

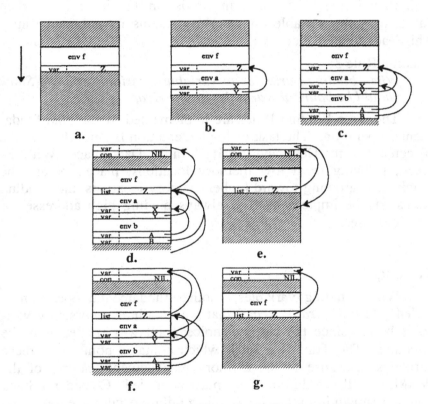

Figure 2.15: Binding Heap and Stack variables

however, it will have deallocated its environment. This will leave Z bound to a list containing a variable pointing to a deactivated and possibly reclaimed area on the Stack as shown in Figure 2.15e.

The correct binding is shown in Figure 2.15f after "d" is invoked showing the dereferenced value of "A" (X in "a") bound to the newly created variable in the list on the Heap. Now when "a" returns the variable on the Heap retains its unbound status. This leads to the Rule:

Binding Rule 3:

> *When binding variables to variables, variables on the Stack should be bound to variables on the Heap.*

The three Binding Rules are implemented by the *bind* fundamental operation. The task of implementation is simplified by the placement of the Heap and the Stack in the Data Space. With the Heap, growing from low memory locations, placed before the Stack, also growing toward higher memory locations, the Binding Rules can be implemented by always binding high addresses to low addresses.

Trailing.

When binding variables, another fundamental operation is called into play; *trail*. Recall that when failure occurs, any variables bound since the current choice point was created must be unbound. The Trail is a stack which contains pointers to these variables. Because of the memory management features of the WAM, not all variable bindings must be trailed. Consider a Stack segment shown in Figure 2.16a When failure occurs, the top of the Stack is restored to the choice point at B. The E register will also be restored from the choice point to a value pointing to an environment before the choice point. Therefore any variable bindings in environments "c" and "d" need not be trailed since this Stack area will be reclaimed during failure. Likewise on the Heap, shown in Figure 2.16b, failure will restore the top of the Heap as indicated

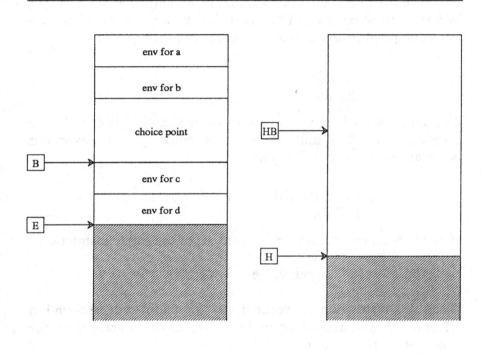

a. Stack   **b. Heap**

Figure 2.16: The Stack for Trailing Variables

by the HB register. Therefore variables bound between HB and H need not be trailed. Otherwise, variable bindings must be trailed to be undone on backtracking. This observation leads to a trail decision as follows:

Trail Rule

If a variable is being bound on the Stack before B or on the Heap before HB, push the variable location on the Trail.

General Unification.

The final fundamental operation is the *unify* operation. In the WAM, unification is often accomplished by a sequence of instructions compiled from the Prolog source. For example:

f :- g(X).
g([a,b,c]).

The unification of the variable X to the list [a, b, c] is done by the instructions for head unification for procedure "g". However, this is not always the case. Consider

f :- g(f(a, [b], X), f(Y, [W], c)).
g(Z,Z).

Here the head unification for "g" consists of the single instruction

get_value   X1,X2

When this instruction is executed, two structures will be found in X1 and X2 which must be unified. Therefore, a general unifier must also be provided in the WAM.

This unifier may be defined as follows:

DEFINITION

To unify X and Y

Rule 1: If X and Y are constants, match X and Y.

Rule 2: If X is a variable or Y is a variable, bind X and Y according to the Binding Rules.

Rule 3: If X and Y are both lists, unify each element of X with the corresponding element of Y

Rule 4: If X and Y are both structures, match the functors of X and Y and unify each element of X with the corresponding element of Y

The recursive nature of Rules 3 and 4 call for the use of the PDL to store intermediate positions in the compound terms being unified.

CHAPTER SUMMARY

This Chapter has described an abstract machine for compiling and executing Prolog programs defined by Warren [63]. The data types and memory organization have been described and some basic terminology has been provided. The instruction set defined by Warren was described in detail and the protocols and fundamental operations used by the instructions were specified.

This specification for an abstract Prolog machine is taken as the starting point for the extensions and enhancements defined in the next Chapter.

CHAPTER 3

A MODIFIED WAM

THE PLM

This Chapter discusses the evolution of the Warren Abstract Machine described in Chapter 2 toward a physical machine, the Prolog Machine, PLM, described in Chapter 4. Given the instruction set of the WAM and the data types on which it processes, specific representations for both code and data are first described. Then new instructions and enhancements of old instructions are proposed. As part of this discussion the issue of built-in predicates in Prolog is identified as one of the major missing elements in the WAM specification and is addressed as a prominent feature of the PLM. Finally, some of the issues of compiling Prolog to run on the PLM are discussed.

Before delving into the specifics of the PLM Instruction Set Architecture (ISA), a "big picture" of the system architecture would be helpful. As was discussed in Chapter 1, the trend in architectures of computing systems has been toward specialized functional units and, more recently, coprocessors for specific segments of the total problem. The PLM is designed as a loosely-coupled, specialized coprocessor for symbolic computing. As such the PLM works together with another processor (or processors) referred to here as the host. Figure 3.1 shows one configuration of a system incorporating the PLM.

The PLM engine (a modified WAM and the subject of this Chapter), interfaces through the PLM Memory Interface (PMI [65]) and a bus interface unit (BIU) to a system bus. The bus provides access to services such as memory, Input/Output, Floating Point computations, and other host support operations. The

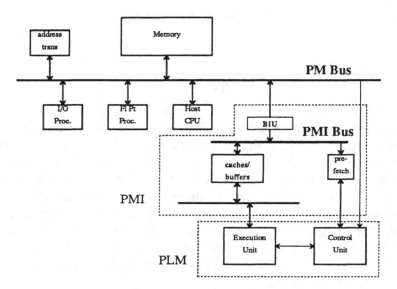

Figure 3.1: Block Diagram of a PLM System

elements of the PMI are described in detail in Chapter 4.

The PLM engine is designed as a 32 bit processor with tag support and specialized hardware and microcode. Figure 3.2 shows the complete instruction set of the PLM. The additions, deletions and modifications of the WAM instructions in the Figure are discussed below.

Finally, several of the examples used in this Chapter are taken from the benchmark programs used to test the PLM.

Procedure Control		Get	
try	L	get_variable	Vi,Ai
retry	L	get_value	Vi,Ai
trust	L	get_constant	C,Ai
try_me_else	L	get_list	Ai
retry_me_else	L	get_structure	F,Ai
trust_me_else	fail	get_nil	Ai
cut			
cutd	L		
fail			
nop			
Indexing		Put	
switch_on_term	Lc,Ll,Ls	put_variable	Vi,Ai
switch_on_constant	n,ff	put_value	Vi,Ai
switch_on_structure	n,ff	put_unsafe_value	Yi,Ai
		put_constant	C,Ai
		put_list	Ai
		put_structure	F,Ai
		put_nil	Ai
Clause Control		Unify	
call	P,n	unify_variable	Vi
execute	P	unify_value	Vi
proceed		unify_constant	C
escape	BI	unify_cdr	Vi
allocate		unify_nil	
deallocate		unify_void	N

Figure 3.2: The PLM Instruction Set

ADDRESS SPACE OF THE PLM

Like the WAM the memory space of the PLM is divided into two major distinct areas, the Code Space and the Data Space. The Code Space contains the PLM instructions which constitute procedures, and clauses. The instruction set has no direct access to the Code Space for writing. Such access is provided via the loader software in the host and via the *assert* and *retract* built-in predicates also implemented externally. Read access to the Code Space is restricted to instruction fetch operations (done by the Prefetch Unit) and hash table accesses by some indexing instructions. Addresses in the Code Space are 30 bit byte addresses providing a 1 gigabyte virtual address space for code. Instruction formats and organization are described below.

The Data Space is further divided into three areas as in the WAM; the Heap, the Stack, and the Trail. All items in the Data Space are 32 bits and those on the Heap and in the permanent variable section of environments on the Stack are 32 bit tagged data representations. Access in the Data Space is via 28 bit word addresses providing a 1 gigabyte virtual address space for data.

Representing Data.

The four data types of the WAM are implemented as shown in Figure 3.3. Two primary tag bits identify the data type. In addition, a cdr-bit (described below) and a single bit for use by an external garbage collection mechanism are provided. The garbage collector is not currently implemented in the PLM and will not be discussed further here. The data types are as follows:

Reference(Data<31:30> = 10)

These data items are used to represent Prolog variables. A variable may be either unbound or bound to the value of another data item in the Data Space. The representation of Reference items includes a tag field and a pointer value. For a bound variable, the pointer value is the address of the binding which itself may be a variable (bound or unbound) or a non-variable data item. An unbound variable contains a pointer to itself. (Note: this restricts variables to "live" in memory, not in registers. A register containing a variable has a pointer to memory.)

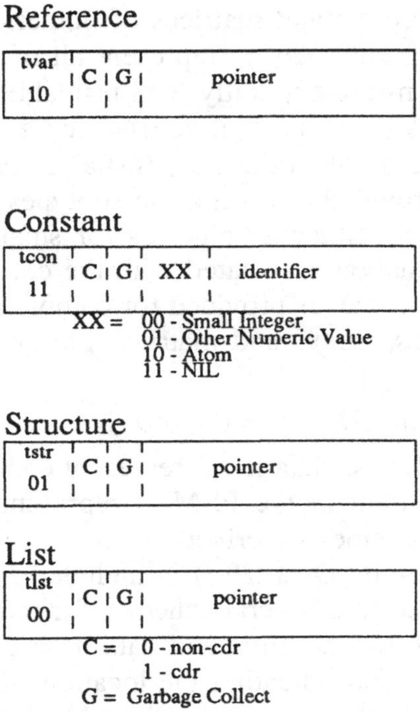

Reference

```
┌──────┬───┬───┬─────────────────────┐
│ tvar │ C │ G │                     │
│  10  │   │   │       pointer       │
└──────┴───┴───┴─────────────────────┘
```

Constant

```
┌──────┬───┬───┬────┬────────────────┐
│ tcon │ C │ G │ XX │   identifier   │
│  11  │   │   │    │                │
└──────┴───┴───┴────┴────────────────┘
```
XX = 00 - Small Integer
      01 - Other Numeric Value
      10 - Atom
      11 - NIL

Structure

```
┌──────┬───┬───┬─────────────────────┐
│ tstr │ C │ G │                     │
│  01  │   │   │       pointer       │
└──────┴───┴───┴─────────────────────┘
```

List

```
┌──────┬───┬───┬─────────────────────┐
│ tlst │ C │ G │                     │
│  00  │   │   │       pointer       │
└──────┴───┴───┴─────────────────────┘
```
C = 0 - non-cdr
     1 - cdr
G = Garbage Collect

Figure 3.3: PLM Data Types.

Constant (Data<31:30> = 11)

These data items represent various constants in Prolog. The instruction set treats all constants in the same manner regardless of what they represent (with the single exception of the constant NIL). However, the programmer has a collection of built-in functions available which can distinguish and operate on constants based on their meaning. Constants may be further divided into numeric and non-numeric. Non-numeric constants are atomic symbols used in Prolog including a unique atom for NIL. Numeric constants include representations for integers and floating point values, as well as vectors and matrices of numeric values. Since 26 bits is not always sufficient to represent all of the information associated with a constant explicitly (e.g. printable form of atoms, or IEEE Floating Point values), a constant data item includes a subtype tag field and an identifier field (Data<25:0>). Two bits of secondary tag are provided to distinguish subtypes (Data<27:26>). The identifier may be either a value, as for small integers, or a pointer to the information associated with the constant. The subtype "other numeric value" is provided for completeness, however, Floating Point values, arrays and matrices are not currently supported in the PLM.

Compound Data(Data<31:30> = 00 or 01)

Like the WAM these data items represent compound terms of Prolog. Compound data in the PLM is represented using a list based cdr-coded scheme described below. To support this representation, a cdr-bit (Data<29>) is included in each word in the Data Space. There are several schemes for representing compound data. In all cases, a compound data item consists of a tag field and a pointer value indicating the location of the compound item (on the Heap). The first scheme, utilized by Tick and Warren, [57] is a structure-based representation. Here a structure is represented as a block of contiguous words in the Data Space, the first of which is the functor and arity (typically in one word - a special atomic form) with the remaining words containing the elements. Lists are represented as a collection of structures. Each element of a list is a structure of arity 2 whose primary functor is dot (.). The first element of the structure, the *car*, contains the list element and the second element, the *cdr*, generally indicates the remainder of the list. The *cdr* may also contain the constant NIL indicating the end of the list (or any arbitrary constant as in the list [a | b]), or may be a Reference data item indicating an unknown list tail ([a | X]). This is the traditional *cons* cell representation of

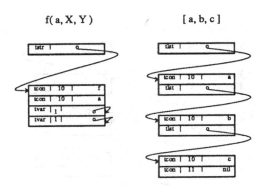

Figure 3.4: Structure Based Representation.

lists used in LISP. For data compression and efficiency, a separate primary tag value is assigned to lists and the functor/arity omitted from memory. Figure 3.4 shows an example of a structure and a list using this scheme assuming all variables are unbound.

A second scheme, based on the LISP *cons* cell, is a list-based representation. Here the primary compound data item is the list cell consisting of two contiguous Data Space locations representing the *car* and the *cdr*. Lists are represented directly, and a structure may be represented as a list whose first element is the functor and the remaining elements are the elements of the list. Again a separate primary tag is provided for structures to indicate that the first element is a functor. Figure 3.5 shows the examples of Figure 3.4 using the list based scheme.

A comparison of these two schemes shows that lists are represented the same way under both schemes, but structures require twice as much storage for the list-based representation even though the cells are contiguous making structure based f(a, X, Y)   [a, b, c]

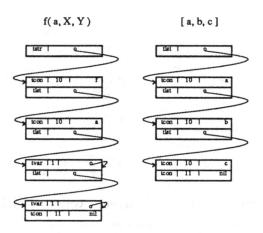

Figure 3.5: List Based Representation.

representations superior. Ideally, a combination of these schemes may provide the advantages of both without the disadvantages of either.

Such a scheme is based on cdr-coding similar to schemes utilized in several LISP Processors. The cdr-coding scheme used in the PLM is somewhat unique in its use of a single cdr-bit rather than two or more bits as in many LISP cdr-coding schemes (c.f. Bobrow and Clark [6]). Similar single bit schemes have been proposed for LISP by Hansen [27] and more recently Li and Hudak [37]. In general, there are two possibilities for encoding the cdr information: in the car element of the list or in the cdr element. For reasons made clear later in this Chapter, the PLM choses the later. Under this scheme, each memory element is identified as to its use as a *car* item or as a *cdr* item. For compact list representation, the list elements normally in the *car* fields are stored

consecutively in memory whenever possible. Cdr-cells need only
be present when required by a discontinuity in memory locations.
Figure 3.6 shows the examples of Figure 3.4 under this scheme.
Note that structures require the same amount of storage as in the
structure-based representation, and that lists do not have a unique
representation. Two of the possible representations of this example are shown in the Figure. In its most compact form, called cdr-
compressed, a list requires about half of the storage of the other
schemes; while in the worst case, with all cdr elements present

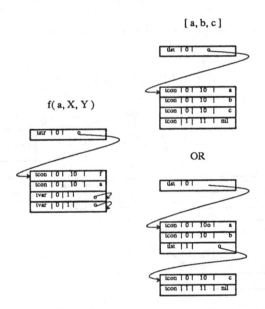

Figure 3.6: Cdr-Coded Representation.

called cdr-expanded, a list requires the same storage as the other schemes. Since the cdr of a list may be any arbitrary Prolog data item (not necessarily a list), a cdr field is provided in all data type representations.

A more complicated list is shown in partially cdr-expanded form in Figure 3.7. Here the list represented is:

$$[[a, b], c, [d], e | X]$$

Note that the list tagged items without the cdr-bit set represent the nested lists while those with the cdr-bit set are list cdr pointers.

$$[[a, b], c, [d], e \quad | X]$$

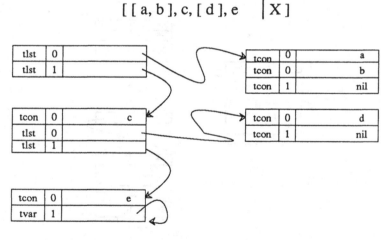

Figure 3.7: A More Complex List Represented

Note also that this list is terminated with an unbound cdr variable.

Representing Code.

The Code Space of the PLM is byte addressable to allow compact storage of compiled and assembled Prolog programs and to minimize the need for bus bandwidth for fetching code from memory. A PLM instruction is assembled into one of six formats as shown in Figure 3.8a. An instruction consists of a one byte opcode followed by 0,1,2, or 3 arguments. The first argument may be either a single byte or a full 32 bit quantity (byte aligned). Arguments 2 and 3, if present, are always a single byte each. Single byte arguments may represent a register specifier (AX or Y, distinguished by the opcode) or a P relative offset for branching. The 32 bit arguments may represent either a fully tagged data item for literals in the instruction stream or a 30 bit absolute byte address in the Code Space for branching. Figure 3.8b shows the two formats for instructions as partially decoded and aligned by the Prefetch Unit and fed to the PLM. This operation will be described in the next Chapter.

The opcode assignments for the PLM are made to simplify the partial decode operation performed by the Prefetch Unit and the decode done by the PLM at instruction boundaries. The format for the opcode is:

7	6	5	4	3	2	1	0
J	Size			B/Y	S	Ident	

The opcodes include an explicit 3 bit field describing the size of the instruction. This field contains the number of bytes which follow the opcode. Figure 3.9 shows the instruction set, with opcode assignments, broken down by size. The J (Jump) bit signifies

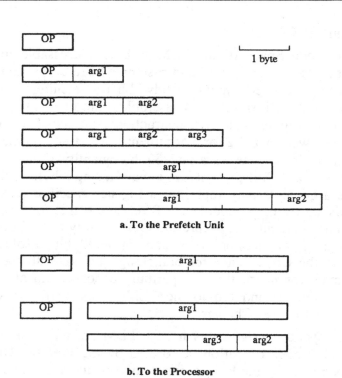

a. To the Prefetch Unit

b. To the Processor

Figure 3.8: Instruction Formats.

Size 0		Size 1		Size 2	
00	allocate	10	get_nil	20	get_variable X
01	deallocate	11	get_list	21	get_value X
02	unify_nil	12	put_nil	22	put_variable X
0b	trust_me_else fail	13	put_list	23	put_value X
04	nop	14	unify_cdr X	28	get_variable Y
05	cut	15	unify_variable X	29	get_value Y
80	proceed	17	unify_value X	2a	put_variable Y
82	fail	18	unify_void	2b	put_value Y
		1c	unify_cdr Y	2c	put_unsafe_value
		1d	unify_variable Y		
		1f	unify_value Y		

Size 3		Size 4		Size 5	
b4	switch_on_term	40	unify_constant	50	get_constant
		41	try_me_else	51	get_structure
		42	retry_me_else	52	put_constant
		44	execute	53	put_structure
		45	try	54	call
		46	retry	d0	switch_on_constant
		47	trust	d1	switch_on_structure
		49	cutd		
		4a	escape		

Figure 3.9: Opcode Assignment.

instructions which must stall the Prefetch Unit for changes in control flow dependent on data only available when the instruction is executed. This feature is described in the next Chapter. The B/Y bit serves a dual purpose depending on the size of the instruction. For size 1 and 2 instructions it signifies that arg1 is a Y register specifier. For size 3 and 4 instructions it signifies an external operation request. (At present only **escape** uses the B bit this way.

Instructions for a tightly coupled coprocessor could be encoded with the B bit). The S bit is used by size 4 and 5 instructions to indicate a swap operation to be performed by the Prefetch Unit to follow control flow changes in the code. (This feature is described in the next Chapter). The remaining bits of the opcode distinguish individual instructions.

COMPLETING THE INSTRUCTION SET

The design of the PLM instruction set began with that of the WAM. However, not all of the functionality of Prolog is supported by the WAM instruction set. This section describes the additional instructions of the PLM to support the *cut* operation as well as an instruction to support the cdr-coded representation of compound terms in the PLM. An instruction to support Prolog built-in predicates is described in a later section. Finally, a discussion of an unnecessary instruction is presented.

Support for cdr-coding.

The cdr-coded representation of compound data in the PLM was described earlier. To support this representation, an additional instruction was added; namely **unify_cdr**. With this addition the unify class of instructions may be divided into two groups, those processing the car or information carrying element of a list and those processing the cdr or structural information carrying elements. The division into two groups in the PLM is as follows:

car Processing		cdr Processing	
unify_value	Xi/Yi	unify_cdr	Xi/Yi
unify_variable	Xi/Yi	unify_nil	
unify_constant	C		

This conceptual split in the function of unify instructions allows simplified instruction sequences for processing lists which further supports the choice of a cdr-coded representation over a structure-based. Figure 3.10 shows the instruction sequences for processing the list

[a, b, c]

for both a structure-based and a cdr-coded representation. In the structure based representation, **unify_variable** instructions are required to process the explicit, always present cdr of a list element as in Figure 3.10a. In the cdr-coded scheme, the instruction sequence need only process the data elements of the list, leaving the structural processing to the underlying implementation of these instructions. In particular, the car processing instructions know they are to unify only with information carrying elements. If a cdr pointer is encountered in read mode during an attempt to unify with the next element of a list, the implementation must first follow the cdr pointer, an operation called "decdr'ing", before performing the unification. If the cdr element encountered is an unbound variable while processing in read mode, the variable is bound to a cdr-list pointer to the top of the Heap and processing continues in write mode. If a car processing instruction encounters any other cdr-tagged data type in read mode it fails.

It is in write mode where the merits of encoding cdr information in the cdr element is made clear. In write mode car processing instructions simply write their element at the top of the Heap. It is not until a cdr processing instruction is encountered that a cdr-encoding is called for. If this encoding were to be in the car element, the last element written would have to be modified in memory. This is expensive as it involves a memory read/modify/write operation. With the encoding in the cdr element, it can be constructed in the processor before the element is written. Referring to Figure 3.10b, in write mode each of the

---

get_list	A1
unify_constant	a
unify_variable	X4
get_list	X4
unify_constant	b
unify_variable	X4
get_list	X4
unify_variable	c
unify_nil	

a : Structure-Based.

get_list	A1
unify_constant	a
unify_constant	b
unify_constant	c
unify_nil	

b : Cdr-Coded.

Figure 3.10: Instruction Sequences

---

unify_constant instructions does not know if an explicit cdr element is to follow so it must write its element without a cdr-bit set. When the **unify_nil** instruction is executed, the explicit cdr is specified but the constant **c** has already been written. In read mode there is little difference for placement of the cdr encoding. The decdr operation can take place either before unification (to find the car element to unify) or after unification (to update the pointer for the next instruction). A slight performance gain might be realized in the later case if part of the decdr operation can overlap the unification but the losses in write mode in this case would be greater.

The cdr processing instructions, on the other hand, do not decdr before attempting to unify. The **unify_nil** instruction expects the next memory location to be a cdr-tagged data item which will unify with NIL. (This could be either the constant NIL itself or a cdr-tagged variable). The **unify_cdr** instruction must be a little more intelligent. If the next memory location is cdr-tagged, the operation is to copy this data item (without its cdr tag) into its operand register. However, if the next location is not cdr-tagged, (i.e. the list is cdr-compressed at this point) the **unify_cdr** instruction must create a new list pointer to this location. It should be noted that the **unify_cdr** instruction processes in the "variable" sense, i.e. it initializes a register to the value without doing a unification. This frees the **unify_variable** instruction from doing double duty to process variables in car and cdr positions. It would also be possible to include instructions such as **unify_cdr_value** and **unify_cdr_constant** for use when information is also stored in the cdr fields of lists (as in dotted pair storage used for A-lists in LISP). However, with the Prolog structure data type and the PLM cdr-coded lists, the need for such a construct is not great. In instances where it is used, a sequence of a **unify_cdr** instruction followed by an appropriate get instruction will do the unification.

For example, unifying the list

[a | b]

would be compiled as

```
get_list         Xi
unify_constant   a
unify_cdr        Xj
get_constant     b,Xj
```

An analysis of the effects of cdr-coding is provided in Chapter 5.

The cut Operation.

In the Prolog model of execution and the abstract machine discussed in Chapter 2, Prolog is described as a language for exploring a search space for the solution to a query. The abstract instruction set provides the mechanisms for control of this search over the space defined by the logic specification provided by the programmer. In practical Prolog systems, however, it is found that more efficient execution can be realized when the programmer is given the capability of influencing the control element of the program. The primary construct for such control provided in Prolog is the *cut* operation (!). With a *cut* the programmer can tell the system that the solution or partial solution to the current subgoal found thus far is sufficient, and further exploration of the search tree below this point for alternate solutions should not be done. Clocksin and Mellish [13] provide an excellent description of *cut* and its uses. In terms of the execution model of the WAM, the search tree pruning effect of *cut* can be realized by pruning choice points from the stack. In his early work on a Prolog instruction set, Warren [63] briefly describes this operation. However, the WAM as defined in [64] does not address the *cut* operation. To provide for *cut* in the PLM, two instructions have been added to the WAM instruction set, **cut** and **cutd**.

The common uses of the *cut* operation (!) are provided by the **cut** instruction. Under the semantics of ! in these cases, the operation to be performed by the **cut** instruction is to remove any and all choice points on the stack associated with the current procedure and with the procedures invoked as subgoals up to the point of the *cut* by the current clause. This can be made clear with an example:

(1)   a :- b,c.
(2)   a :- ...
 .
 .
 .
(3)   c :- e,!,f.
(4)   c :- g,!,h.

In this example the procedure "a" will have a choice point on the stack when executing clause (1). When procedure "c" is invoked as a subgoal and clause (3) is tried a choice point will be created for "c" indicating clause (4) as the failure address. When the ! is executed in clause (3) procedure "e" and its descendants may or may not have choice points on the stack. The semantics of ! say to remove all choice points associated with "e" and its descendants and the choice point associated with "c". Thus after the **cut** instruction the current choice point (top choice point on the stack) should be that associated with procedure "a" (assuming "b" has no alternate clauses). If instead procedure "c" tries clause (4), the **cut** instruction here should remove any and all choice points associated with "g" and its descendants. However in this case, procedure "c" no longer has a choice point on the stack to be removed as (4) is the last alternative for procedure "c". Again the effect of ! is to make the current choice point that of "a". The code for procedure "c" would be:

```
            try_me_else   L1
            allocate
            {gets for c head}
            {puts for e}
            call              e,n
            cut
            {puts for f}
            deallocate
            execute                     f


    L1:     trust_me_else fail
            allocate
            {gets for c head}
            {puts for g}
            call              g,n
            cut
            {puts for h}
            deallocate
            execute                     h
```

The implementation of the **cut** instruction must identify the choice point which is to become current and update the B register to indicate this action. To do this, another item is added to the static area of the environment, namely the value of the B register (a pointer to the current choice point) at the time the environment is created. Then **cut** can simply reload the B register from this field when it is executed (see Figure 3.11a). This provides correct operation in the case of clause (4) above since the current choice point is that associated with "a" when the environment of (4) is created. However, for the ! in clause (3) the B register value stored in the environment indicates the choice point of procedure "c" which must also be removed by again reloading the B register from the value stored in this choice point (see Figure 3.11b). To cover both of these cases, the **cut** instruction must be able to determine if there is a choice point on the stack associated with the current procedure. To do this, a single bit flag, called the cut flag,

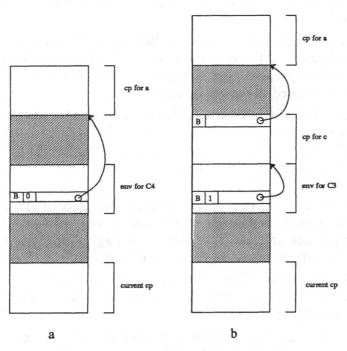

Figure 3.11: A Snapshot of the Stack.

is added to the architecture. Whenever a choice point is created (**try** or **try_me_else**) the cut flag is set. When a choice point is removed (**trust** or **trust_me_else**) the cut flag is reset. In addition, whenever a subgoal is invoked (**call** or **execute**) the cut flag is reset to validate its value for the invoked procedure (i.e. the invoked procedure has no choice point on the stack). When the B register is stored in the environment the current value of the cut flag is stored with it. The algorithm for the **cut** instruction becomes:

(1)   Access the current environment for the B register value and cut flag stored there. Update the B register from this value.

(2)   If the stored cut flag is set, access the choice point now indicated by the B register for the B register value stored there and update the B register again. Reset the cut flag value stored in the environment.

The update of the stored cut flag in 2) is done for clauses with more than one cut.

(5)   a :- b, c, !, d, e, !, f.
(6)   a :- ...

Here the first cut will remove the choice point associated with "a" so that the second need only remove those associated with "d" and "e" and their descendants. The stored cut flag in the environment for "a" must reflect this when the first ! is executed.

It should be noted that the presence of a ! in a clause requires that an environment be allocated for a clause even if there are no permanent variables in the clause.

There is one other instance of the use of ! not handled by the **cut** instruction; namely cuts in disjunctions. The most common example of this is the *if-then-else* construct provided by Prolog:

(7)   (a -> b; c)

This can be read as "if a is true then b else c", and is equivalent to

(8)   (a, !, b; c)

(see Van Roy [61]).

By the semantics of disjunction (;) a choice point must be created on the stack to sequence through the disjuncts on failure. The semantics of the ! in (8) are to remove any choice points associated with "a" and its descendants and the choice point for the disjunction. Since only one environment can be allocated for a clause, the implementation of ! in (8) cannot use the **cut** instruction. For this case the **cutd** instruction is added to the ISA. The compiled code for (8) is:

```
            ...
            try_me_else   L1
            {puts for a}
            call          a,n
            cutd          L1
            {puts for b}
            call          b,n
            execute             L2
      L1:   trust_me_else fail
            {puts for c}
            call          c,n
      L2:   ...
```

The **cutd** instruction has a label as its operand and its semantics are as follows:

(1)   Access the failure address in the current choice point. If this address matches the operand address remove the choice point (update the B and HB registers from the choice point) and proceed to the next instruction.

(2)   Otherwise, remove the choice point and repeat 1).

The effect of **cutd** is to walk back up the choice point stack until the desired choice point is found, removing choice points along the way. This could be a much more expensive operation than **cut** which can access the desired choice point directly without looking at any intermediate choice points on the stack.

It can be noted that the **cutd** instruction can also be used to implement the standard *cut* operation in all cases except cuts in the last clause of a procedure (e.g. clause (4) above). For example, the code for clause (3) above could be compiled as

```
try_me_else    L1
allocate
{gets for c head}
puts for e}
call           e,n
cutd           L1
{puts for f}
deallocate
execute                    f
```

This cannot be done for clause (4) since the label operand for the **cut** in clause (4) cannot be identified at compile time. It could possibly be any label associated with clauses in procedure "d" or, worse, a procedure above "c" in the dynamic search tree in which case it should not be removed as dictated by the semantics of **cutd**. Even if this obstacle could be overcome, the chain of choice points from the current to the target may be very long. This makes all cuts potentially very expensive at run time thus the **cut** instruction provides an efficient mechanism for the normal *cut* construct.

One additional use can be made of the **cutd** instruction, namely for implementing the idea of soft cuts (sometimes called snips [31]) suggested as an augmentation of control constructs for Prolog. For example in the clause

(9)   a :- b, c, [!, d, e, !], f.

the predicate [! indicates the generation of a soft cut point. When the predicate !] is executed, choice points associated with "d", "e" and their descendants are to be removed as well as the soft cut point. The compiled code for this clause would be:

```
                {gets for a head}
                {puts for b}
                call            b,n
                {puts for c}
                call            c,n
                try_me_else     L1      % create soft cut point
                {puts for d}
                call            d,n
                {puts for e}
                call            e,n
                cutd            L1      % soft cut
                {puts for f}
                execute                 f
        L1:     trust_me_else fail
                fail
```

The **cutd** instruction performs exactly the desired operation of soft cut. The code at label L1 is provided should execution ever fail to the soft cut point. This code removes the soft cut choice point and fails to propagate the failure back up the dynamic search tree.

Finally, one other instruction may be used to implement the *cut* operation; **trust_me_else fail**. Recall this instruction removes the top choice point from the Stack. It is more efficient than either of the cut instructions as no tests are done; only a single choice point is removed. This instruction may be used to implement *cut* when the compiler can identify that only a single choice point need be removed. An example can be seen in the clause fragment

$$..., (X < 0, !, a; b), ...$$

Here the "less than" subgoal before the disjunctive cut does not create any choice points so the *cut* must remove only the choice point for the disjunction. The compiled code is:

```
            ...
            try_me_else     L1      % disjunctive choice point
            put_value       Xi,X1   % value of X
            put_constant    0,X2
            escape          <
            trust_me_else   fail    % cut
            {puts for a}
            call            a,n
            execute                 L2
      L1:
            trust_me_else   fail    % remove disjunctive choice po
            {puts for b}
            call            b,n
      L2:   ...
```

An Unnecessary Instruction.

One instruction provided in the WAM not needed in the PLM is the **unify_local value** instruction. This instruction was intended to handle unsafe variables appearing in compound terms (lists or structures). However, in the PLM this cannot occur. Recall that an unsafe variable is an unbound variable residing in a Y register in the current environment about to be trimmed away. In the PLM the variable binding and creation protocol has all variables on the Stack point to older variables on the Stack or to variables on the Heap (i.e. all variable pointers are to lower memory locations). Therefore a variable in a compound term will reside in the Heap and not be affected by Stack trimming.

In order to enforce this protocol, the **unify_value** instruction in write mode places an unbound variable at the top of the Heap (the next element of the compound term being constructed) and binds this variable to the operand specified by the **unify_value**. The Binding Rules of Chapter 2 then ensure no dangling pointer results when the operand is a local value. Since the **unify_value** instruction in write mode will perform a Heap write in any case, this implementation does not adversely effect the performance.

A similar technique should not be applied to the **put_unsafe_value** instruction since **put_value** would not ordinarily write to the Heap. The added effort to check a variable safe would unnecessarily extend the execution of **put_value** in cases where the compiler can determine a variable is safe. Therefore both **put_value** and **put_unsafe_value** are retained in the PLM.

ENHANCEMENTS TO THE WAM

In addition to completing the instruction set, the PLM modifies the semantics of several WAM instructions to improve performance. This section describes these enhancements.

The Environment Size.

One modification to the WAM concerns the environment size operand of the call instruction. This operand was added by Warren [64] to allow environments to be trimmed dynamically as subgoal processing proceeds from left to right and storage for permanent variables becomes inactive. The original description of this feature did not describe how the value of the operand was obtained when needed to compute the top of the Stack. Recall that the top of the Stack is needed when adding a new environment or choice point and is indicated by the B or E registers. If an environment is currently at the top of the stack, the next available location is past all of the Y registers currently active, i.e. it is E plus the current environment size. One method of determining the environment size is to access the operand from the **call** instruction in the Code Space when needed. Since the CP register indicates the return point from the call, the location of the operand could be calculated. For the PLM, however, the Code Space is byte aligned where the normal path to memory is for word aligned 32 bit quantities. (This is even true for instruction fetching as will be seen when the Prefetch Unit is discussed). Therefore the extraction of environment size dynamically from the Code Space would be difficult.

In the PLM, environment trimming is handled by adding a register to the processor, the N register, loaded by the **call** instruction. Thus the environment size is readily available in a processor register when required. Since the size varies for each call as inference depth increases and must be restored upon return, the N register value is stacked by adding it to the status area of the environment; N is saved by the allocate instruction and restored by deallocate.

Indexing Instructions.

Several slight modifications have been made to the WAM indexing instructions. The **switch_on_term** instruction has been shortened to three operands, for constant, list and structure cases with the variable case defaulting to the following instruction. The three arguments are each one byte in length representing a P relative address offset. This restricts the target address to 255 bytes away (HEX ff indicates failure). However the assembler can easily rearrange code so that the target will always be within range. One form of the procedure code after rearrangement would appear as follows:

	switch_on_term	Lc,Ll,Ls
Lv:	execute	C1a
Lc:	switch_on_constant	Hc,nc
Ls:	switch_on_structure	Hs,ns
Ll:	try	Cx
	retry	Cy
	...	
	trust	Cz
% Hash Tables		
Hc:	constant1	CLabel1
	constant2	CLabel2
	...	
	constantnc	CLabelnc
Hs:	functor1	FLabel1
	functor2	FLabel2
	...	
	functorns	FLabelns
% Clause Code		
C1a:	try_me_else	C2a
	...	
C2a:	retry_me_else	C3a
	..	

For the hashing instructions, **switch_on_constant** and **switch_on_structure**, a very simple hashing scheme is used in the PLM. The second argument is a one byte mask 'ANDED' with the constant or functor being hashed to provide an offset into the hash table indicated by the first argument. These instructions then verify a hit by comparing the hashed value with the stored value, branching to the stored label on success. Rehashing consists of a linear probing of the table (wrapping around if necessary). The last valid entry in the table is tagged with a cdr bit set in the label field to identify when wrapping around to the beginning of the table is required. The unused table entries are padded with NIL to indicate failure should initial hashing fall in such an area.

One further problem concerning the hashing instructions
relates to how these instructions are used in generating procedure
code. Recall that the **switch_on_term** instruction identifies four
blocks of procedure code based on the type of the first argument of
the invoking query, the variable block (all clauses must be tried),
the list block (only clauses with variable or list first parameters if
their heads need be tried), and the constant and structure blocks.
These last two blocks are similar and may use hashing instructions
to further filter the clauses. There are two ways of generating code
for these blocks as can best be seen from an example. Consider
the following procedure "f" with eight clauses: (The clause bodies
are not important for describing procedure code).

$$
\begin{array}{ll}
\text{C1:} & \text{f(X) :-} \\
\text{C2:} & \text{f(a) :-} \\
\text{C3:} & \text{f(a) :-} \\
\text{C4:} & \text{f(a) :-} \\
\text{C5:} & \text{f(b) :-} \\
\text{C6:} & \text{f(Y) :-} \\
\text{C7:} & \text{f(c) :-} \\
\text{C8:} & \text{f(d) :-}
\end{array}
$$

Figure 3.12a shows the constant block code generated by creating
a choice point and inserting a hashing instruction where a
sequence of clauses have constant first parameters. This seems the
obvious way to compile the procedure code when scanning down
the clauses of the procedure. However, notice that in the case of
an invoking constant **a**, two choice points are created for the procedure, the first to sequence the two variable cases with the constant case and the second to sequence between the three constant **a**
clauses. Figure 3.12b shows the constant block code generated by
first hashing on the constant to identify a try-block (c.f. Van Roy
etal. [62]) for each constant appearing in the procedure. Each of
these four try-blocks then generate a single choice point and
sequence the entire subset of clauses which could unify with the

	try	C1		switch_on_constant	T,3
	retry_me_else	L	T:	a	La
	switch_on_constant	T1,1		b	Lb
T1:	a	La		c	Lc
	b	C5		d	Ld
L:	retry	C6	La:	try	C1
	trust_me_else	fail		retry	C2
	switch_on_constant	T2,1		retry	C3
T2:	c	C7		retry	C4
	d	C8		trust	C6
La:	try	C2	Lb:	try	C1
	retry	C3		retry	C5
	trust	C4		trust	C6
			Lc:	try	C1
				retry	C6
				trust	C7
			Ld:	try	C1
				retry	C6
				trust	C8

a	b

Figure 3.12: Constant Block Code.

invoking constant argument.

The difference between the two methods of compiling constant block code is due to the fact that the subsets of clauses to be tried for each invoking constant argument are not disjoint. They intersect for clauses with variable first parameters. The first method minimizes the static amount of code generated by using a common instruction for each of these intersection points. The second method generates more static code; however, the code executed at run-time is at most the same, and in the case of procedure "f" above, less, since no second choice point need be generated. (Choice point creation is an expensive operation).

However, there remains an objection to the code in Figure 3.12b. What if the procedure were invoked with a constant not appearing in the clause heads? For example

$$...,f(e),...$$

Since **e** does not hash to any entry in the hash table, the **switch_on_constant** instruction fails causing procedure "f" to fail and backtrack further up the tree. This is incorrect. In this case clauses C1 and C6 should be tried as would happen in the code in Figure 3.12a. This situation can be remedied by specifying that should a constant not appear in a hash table, a default instruction should be executed instead of failing. The obvious default instruction is the one immediately following the switch_on_constant. The constant block for "f" would then become:

```
              switch_on_constant    T,3
              try                   C1 % not in table
              trust                 C6
      T:      a                     La
              b                     Lb
              c                     Lc
              d                     Ld
      La:     try                   C1 % constant a
              retry                 C2
              retry                 C3
              retry                 C4
              trust                 C6
      Lb:     try                   C1 % constant b
              retry                 C5
              trust                 C6
      Lc:     try                   C1 % constant c
              retry                 C6
              trust                 C7
      Ld:     try                   C1 % constant d
              retry                 C6
              trust                 C8
```

The Van Roy compiler [61] chose the first method for implementing the constant block. However, for the PLM there is one additional complication. In order to implement the cut operation the PLM restricts procedures to at most one choice point. Therefore the Van Roy compiler must modify the way hash tables are generated, prohibiting consecutive clauses with the same constant first parameter from participating in hash filtering operations. The code generated by the compiler is:

	try	C1
	retry	C2
	retry	C3
	retry_me_else	L
	switch_on_constant	T1,1
T1:	a	C4
	b	C5
L:	retry	C6
	trust_me_else	fail
	switch_on_constant	T2,1
T2:	c	C7
	d	C8

Note that with this code if the procedure "f" were invoked as

...,f(b),...

clauses C2 and C3 would be unnecessarily tried (and fail) before the **switch_on_constant** instruction identified clause C5 as the one to try. Van Roy states that this situation does not happen often in Prolog programs [61]. While this is probably true for many applications, it would seem that in a data base application the occurrence of consecutive clauses with the same constant first parameter would be very likely.

An Unnecessary Register.

The original WAM specification included an A register pointing to the top of the Stack. In the WAM model the top of the Stack may be indicated by either the B register if a choice point is at the top or the E register if an environment is at the top. There are four instructions which affect the top of Stack:

Create a Frame	Remove a Frame
allocate	deallocate
try	trust

(actually six but try and try_me_else and trust and trust_me_else are identical for purposes of stack manipulation). With an A register, instructions which create a new stack frame would readily have the top of Stack address available and at most would have to perform an addition (E+N) to put down the new frame and update A. Instructions which remove a frame would have to do a comparison (E vs B) after removing the frame to update A. (This would also apply to cut).

In the PLM this was simplified by removing the A register and having the instructions that create a frame do the comparison and also possibly an addition to determine the top of the stack when needed. Instructions removing a frame need do nothing extra. The comparison and addition can be pipelined in the microcode by doing the addition while making the branch decision based on the compare. This scheme can be further enhanced by enforcing a protocol in the microcode to have E and B readily available for comparison at all instruction boundaries.

Tail Recursion Revisited.

(And a surprise about backtracking). The use of recursion, and particularly tail recursion, in Prolog as well as LISP and other languages provides for elegant and concise statements of a wide variety of algorithms. This section takes a second look at recursion and its implementation on the WAM.

A recursive algorithm takes a form like an inductive proof; an operation or a proof step on one instance of the problem and a recursive invocation on the remaining, simplified instance of the problem. The process concludes with a basis or simplest form of the problem, namely the terminating condition. An example will clarify. Figure 3.13a shows the Prolog code for appending two lists to form a third. The second clause copies one element of the first list to the result and recurs for the remainder of the first list. The terminating condition is when the first list is empty where the first clause appends the second list to the end of the result list. The compiled code for the PLM is shown in Figure 3.13b. The **switch_on_term** instruction is used to test for termination. As is the case for any implementation of recursion, this test is performed for each recursive call. The search tree diagram for append is shown in Figure 3.14. It should be noted that the code for the AND nodes in the non-determinate case is identical to the AND nodes for the determinate case.

As an alternative, note that the **get-list** instruction in the code for C2 can also be used to test for termination, producing a failure when the first list is empty. Thus the code for the determinate recursive step can branch to itself rather than execute the **switch_on_term** test in the OR node. This is shown in the code in Figure 3.15 and the diagram in Figure 3.16. At first glance there are two problems with this implementation of append. The first has to do with performance. With the code in Figure 3.15 a single choice point is created for append even in the determinate case, and a failure operation is performed where none was before. Since these operations involve saving and restoring processor state, both expensive (time consuming) operations, this "enhancement" would seem to hinder rather than improve the performance of append. As will be seen in Chapter 5, in the limit this extra expense is not critical to the performance since it is only incurred once.

The second problem is more serious as it has to do with correctness. Recall the actions taken on failure; restore all processor registers to the values at the invocation of the procedure from the choice point. If this were done, all of the work performed by the AND node for C2 would be undone by the failure. What is needed here is a branch to the alternate clause without state restoration on failure. This is signified by the lateral backtrack arrow

```
append([], L, L).
append([X|L1], L2, [X|L3]) :- append(L1, L2, L3).
```

a. Prolog Code

```
procedure       append
switch_on_term        C1,C2,fail

        try_me_else    C2a
C1:     get_nil         X1              % append( [],
        get_value       X2,X3           % L,L
        proceed                         %      ).

C2a:    trust_me_else  fail
C2:     get_listX1                      % append( [
        unify_variable X4               % X
        unify_cdr      X1               %    |L1], L2,
        get_listX3            %  [
        unify_value    X4               % X
        unify_cdr      X3               %    |L3])
        execute        append           %  :- append(L1,L2,L3).
```

b. PLM Code

Figure 3.13: Code for append

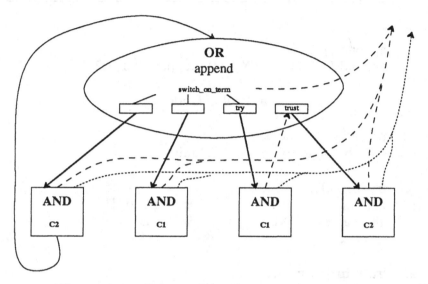

Figure 3.14: Search Tree Diagram for append

```
         procedure append
         switch_on_term        C1,C2,fail

         try_me_else    C2a
C1:      get_nil        X1          %  append( [],
         get_value      X2,X3       %  L,L
         proceed                    %    ).

C2a:     trust_me_else  fail
         get_list       X1                 % append( [
         unify_variable X4          %  X
         unify_cdr      X1          %  |L1],L2,
         get_list       X3              %  [
         unify_value    X4          %  X
         unify_cdr      X3          %  |L3])
         execute               append %  append(L1,L2,L3).

C2:      try_me_else    C1a | tvar  % create short choice point
CC:      get_list       X1                 % append( [
         unify_variable X4          %  X
         unify_cdr      X1          %  |L1],L2,
         get_list       X3              %  [
         unify_value    X4          %  X
         unify_cdr      X3          %  |L3])
         execute               CC   % :- append(L1,L2,L3). (alt)

C1a:     trust          C1          % terminating condition
```

Figure 3.15: Code for Sidetracking append

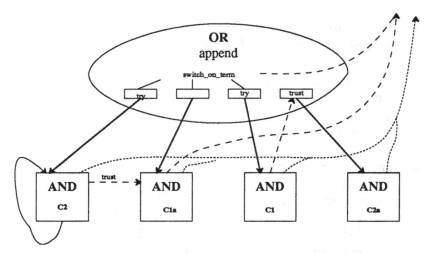

Figure 3.16: Search Tree Diagram for Sidetracking append

in Figure 3.16 giving this technique the name "Sidetracking." Note the **trust** instruction is still required to remove the choice point for the procedure as no alternatives remain. However, it has been moved to the AND node for C1 so that the non-restoring nature of the failure is clear.

With a sidetracking solution to the second problem, the severity of the performance objection can be reduced also. The fail operation is no longer a time consuming restoration of all of the processor state. Only the failure address in the choice point is accessed. For this example, the choice point created by the try instruction does not need to contain the entire processor state. (Note this may not be true in general as the next example will show). If the try instruction is modified to create a short choice point (a short choice point contains only the B and HB entries and the failure address) the performance objection becomes even less convincing. A detailed quantitative analysis of the effects of side-tracking is deferred to Chapter 5. However, it should be obvious that a sidetracking solution can achieve performance at least comparable to one without.

The introduction of sidetracking presents one additional problem. How does a machine differentiate between normal and short choice points and normal and non-restoring failure?

One method of identifying the creation of short choice points is to augment the instruction set with special try and retry instructions. However, this does not inform the fail operation when to do a non-restoring failure. An alternative, shown in Figure 3.15, is to tag the failure address in the **try_me_else** and **retry_me_else** instruction operands which can be tested when the instructions are executed. The tagged values are also stored in the choice point to indicate to **fail** that no registers are to be restored. Since addresses in the Code Space are 30 bit byte addresses, two bits are available to tag the failure address.

The discussion above showed that the sidetracking technique is useful for the tail recursive function *append*. The use of tail recursion, particularly to "cdr down" lists, is common in Prolog. As will be seen in Chapter 5, the sidetracking technique can be applied to other tail recursive procedures. However, there are other uses of sidetracking.

Consider the *split* procedure from the *serialize* benchmark.

```
split([X|L],X,L1,L2)    :- !, split(L,X,L1,L2).
split([X|L],Y,[X|L1],L2) :- before(X,Y),!,
        split(L,Y,L1,L2).
split([X|L],Y,L1,[X|L2]) :- before(Y,X),!,
        split(L,Y,L1,L2).
split([],_,[],[]).
```

This procedure invoked as

?- split(L,X,L1,L2).

will split the list L around the element X into two lists L1 and L2 such that all elements of L1 are less than X and all elements of L2 are greater than X. Duplicates of X are discarded.

First, it is obvious that *split* is tail recursive and therefore sidetracking for tail recursion may be applied. However there is more. To remove the effect of this tail recursion, consider the rewritten form of *split* which uses a separate procedure, *nsplit*.

ssplit([X|L],Y,L1,L2) :- nsplit(L,Y,L1,L2,X).
ssplit([],_,[],[]).

(1)   nsplit(L,X,L1,L2,X) :- !, ssplit(L,X,L1,L2).
(2)   nsplit(L,Y,[X|L1],L2,X) :- before(X,Y), !,
            ssplit(L,Y,L1,L2).
(3)   nsplit(L,Y,L1,[X|L2],X) :- before(Y,X), !,
            ssplit(L,Y,L1,L2).

Now when compiling *nsplit*, it can be noticed that the heads of the three clauses are very similar. With a standard compilation of clauses (2) and (3), get and unify instructions would be used to do head unification, put instructions to arrange registers, and then the call to the first subgoal. In effect, for clause (2), the element X would be added to the list L1 before the test to see if it belongs there. Should the *before* procedure fail, this work would have to be undone (by detrailing bindings and restoring registers) and head unification and register transfers would be repeated for clause (3). With sidetracking, it is possible to avoid this repetition of head unification steps. The compiled code for *nsplit* is shown in Figure 3.17.

The procedure code creates a short choice point and executes clause (1). Should this fail, a short fail operation occurs and the code for clause (2) is executed. Here head unification is deferred, and instead put instructions set up the call to *before*. (Note: the value of Y is saved in register X7 since it is not known that *before*

procedure	nsplit		
	try_me_else	SP3|tvar	% create short choice point
	get_value	X5,X2	
	trust_me_else	fail	% cut
	execute	ssplit	
SP3:	retry_me_else	SP4|tvar	% modify short choice point
	put_value	X1,X6	% L
	put_value	X5,X1	% X
	put_value	X2,X7	% Y
	allocate		
	call	before,0	% test for proper clause
	deallocate		
	trust_me_else	fail	% cut
	put_value	X6,A1	% L
	put_value	X7,A2	% Y
	get_list	X3	% [
	unify_value	X5	% X
	unify_cdr	X3	% |L1]
	execute	ssplit	
SP4:	trust_me_else	fail	% discard short choice point
	put_value	X5,X2	% X
	put_value	X7,X1	% Y
	call	before,0	
	deallocate		
	put_value	X6,A1	% L
	put_value	X7,A2	% Y
	get_list	X4	% [
	unify_value	X5	% X
	unify_cdr	X4	% |L2]
	execute	ssplit	

Figure 3.17: Compiled Code for nsplit

will not modify X2). Only if *before* succeeds will the construction of a list with X and L1 be done. If *before* fails, clause (3) can make use of the register assignments from clause (2) and simply set up registers for its own call to *before*. This is true because no registers are restored on the fail. (The code in Figure 3.17 also assumes that *before* does not modify registers other than X1 and X2. If this assumption could not be made, permanent variables could be used to save X3,X4,X5,X6, and X7 as would be the case for standard compilation. The technique of using temporary variables even across calls is an area for future compiler study).

One additional assumption used in the code of Figure 3.17 is that the third and fourth arguments of *nsplit* are output variables and the first and second are input variables. Such mode information is often available to the compiler or may be generated at compile time.

The separation of sidetracking for tail recursion and sidetracking for deferred head unification does not need to occur. The code for *split* can combine both of these techniques into a single combined procedure. The effects of sidetracking are quantified in Chapter 5.

With the mechanism described here, more complicated uses of sidetracking are possible. For example, a procedure may require deferred head unification through the first several subgoals but full register restoring failure for subsequent subgoals. (This may be the case when subgoals bind variables which then must be unbound on failure). By creating a full choice point and then using **retry_me_else** instructions, the tags of the failure address may be changed at will, switching the mode of failure as necessary. Additional ramifications of sidetracking is an open issue. Some suggestions are discussed in Chapter 6.

IMPLEMENTING BUILT-IN FUNCTIONS

The instruction set designed for the WAM and the extensions discussed so far provide the core of a Prolog system. This includes methods for implementing and manipulating Prolog data types including the single assignment nature of the logical variable in a Prolog clause. Also included are the facilities for the control mechanisms of backtracking to successive clauses in a Prolog procedure and sequencing subgoals within a Prolog clause. In addition, the fundamental operation of unification is supported in the instruction set. However, a complete Prolog implementation must also provide for the built-in predicates of Prolog. These include such operations as Input/Output, arithmetic operations and term comparisons, metalogical operations, and program modification and debugging. This section will address the issues of implementing the built-in predicates in the PLM. Predicates considered here are those described for CProlog [48]. For implementation in the PLM, predicates are divided into three categories: compiler implemented built-ins, internal built-ins, and external built-ins.

Compiler Implemented Built-ins.

Some built-in predicates can be implemented using existing instructions or short sequences of existing instructions (akin to a macro expansion) and are recognized by the compiler. These predicates and their implementation are described by Van Roy [61]. The simplest examples are the conjunction predicate (,) integral to the form of the compiled code and the *true* predicate which requires no code. In addition, the *cut* operator and *fail* predicate are implemented by corresponding instructions.

Other examples include the *unify* predicate (=) which unifys its operands. The **get_value** instruction performs exactly that operation. Also those predicates which test for the existence of a data item of one of the primary PLM data types may be implemented with the **switch_on_term** instruction. For example, the subgoal

$$nonvar(X)$$

is compiled as:

```
switch_on_term Label,Label,Label
fail

Label: ...
```

Predicates *var*, *atomic*, *list*, *structure* and their inverses are compiled similarly.

Finally, some control predicates can be recognized and processed at compile time. These include *repeat* compiled as:

```
        try Label
Label: ...
        fail
```

and various disjunctive forms such as ";", if-then and if-then-else (A -> B and A -> B;C), and *not*. The later are examples of source to source transformations done by the compiler. For example, the subgoal

$$not(X)$$

is transformed to

$$(X \rightarrow fail; true)$$

and subsequently transformed to

$$(X, !, fail; true)$$

A second class of compiler implemented built-ins are those handled by library routines of precompiled Prolog code or specially coded sequences of assembly instructions. Examples include the *sort* and *keysort* predicates, the various program modification predicates (e.g. *assert*, *retract* and *clause*) and program status predicates such as *listing*, *current_atom*, *current_functor*, and *current_predicate*. These library routines may themselves use built-in predicates (e.g. *sort* uses @<). The compiler need do nothing special with these predicates. Their invocation is compiled as a call to a procedure. It is the linker/loader which must ensure that the appropriate library routines are present when the code is loaded into the Code Space.

No special hardware or microcode is needed for the compiler implemented built-ins.

Internal Built-ins.

Some built-ins may be implemented using the functional units provided by the PLM, particularly the ALU. For example, the ALU is capable of doing integer addition and subtraction. Thus special microcode routines are provided to do these operations and some hardware support may be required (e.g. sign extension for integer arithmetic). Other built-ins which can make use of PLM facilities include:

Integer comparison operations (==,=<,>, etc)
Bitwise logical operations ($\wedge, \vee, \setminus$ etc)
Term comparison operations (@<, @>, etc)

The later set of built-ins require that the symbol table (created by the assembler) be ordered in the standard Prolog order.

External Built-ins.

The PLM is designed as a coprocessor working in conjunction with some host processor. Some built-in predicates require the facilities of the host. Examples include:

> Input/Output
> Arithmetic (floating point and some integer, eg multiply)
> Support for debugging
> Support for foreign subroutines

The paradigm chosen for the PLM is that of a loosely-coupled coprocessor. By loosely coupled it is meant that the processors operate on independent instruction streams and that the communication of operands, status and results between processors takes place via shared memory. Under this scheme, an external built-in is invoked by an **escape** instruction in the instruction stream. The operand of the escape identifies the built-in being requested with its arity and the fact that it is external (internal built-ins are also invoked with the **escape** instruction). With this information, the PLM can dump the necessary processor registers and the built-in identifier to a common communication area in memory and interrupt the host to request execution. The registers dumped include the appropriate AX registers (as indicated by the arity), and the H, B, HB, and TR registers. These last registers allow the host to make trail decisions if variables are bound and to add data to the Heap and Trail. Since the Host has access to the entire address space of the PLM, the AX registers, which may contain pointers, are sufficient to communicate operands to the host. Results are returned to the PLM in the form of variable bindings as is the Prolog paradigm. Upon completion of built-in processing, the host indicates the return status in the communication area and signals the PLM to restart. The status signifies the success or failure of the built-in and whether the H and TR registers must be reloaded if entries were made on the Heap or Trail.

Some Particularly Difficult Built-ins.

There are some Prolog built-in predicates that are particularly difficult to implement for compiled code. The first class of these are predicates for modifying the Prolog program, *clause*, *assert* and *retract*. The *assert* and *retract* operations (sometimes referred to as "data base hacking") are believed by many to be an indispensable feature of the language for writing many useful Prolog programs. For a Prolog interpreter clauses may be represented in structure form in the Prolog database and the unification with the source code at run time for *clause* and *retract* is relatively straightforward. In a compiled Prolog system, however, clauses are represented as a block of compiled code. Some form of mapping from the structure form of a clause and its compiled equivalent must be provided for this unification to take place. This section describes the implementation of these operations in the PLM environment described previously. The implementation is based on a collection of library procedures and builtin functions activated via the escape mechanism.

Two forms of *assert* and *retract* operations are described here. The first is only a subset of the full *assert* and *retract* operation and is actually an implementation of global "side-effect" variables which is frequently realized in Prolog using *assert* and *retract*. The implementation here, however, does no actual data base hacking and provides a relatively efficient tool which may be realized by the Prolog functional unit. The second form is an attempt to provide a reasonably full subset of *assert* and *retract* operations for arbitrary clauses and procedures. This form does require manipulation of the Code Space which, as can be seen from the instruction set, is beyond the capabilities of the Prolog functional unit.

Side-effect Variables. A common use of *assert* and *retract* is for implementation of "side-effect" variables in a program. For example, in a branch and bound algorithm a global variable,

cost_bound, may be maintained to keep track of the cost of the best solution found so far. In Prolog, **cost_bound** may be implemented as a single clause procedure, *cost_bound*, consisting of a single fact, the argument of which is the value of the variable. The variable is initialized by the presence of a fact e.g.

cost_bound(32000).

in the original data base. The value of the variable is changed by retracting the *cost_bound* clause and asserting a new one. The variable is accessed by invoking a goal

?- cost_bound(X).

Rather than implement these types of operations using changes to the data base, a pair of builtin functions, *set* and *access*, as well as a non-reclaimable area for global variable storage in the Data Space are provided. In general, *set* is used to both initialize and update the value of a variable; and *access* is used to retrieve the value of a variable. It is the programmer/compiler's responsibility to manage the allocation of the global variable area. The *set* and *access* operations may be defined as follows:

set(loc, value)

where *loc* dereferences to an integer constant corresponding to the word address within the global area to be set.

and   *value* dereferences to the value to be set in the variable.

Set actually places an unbound variable at *loc* and then uses a special unify operation to unify it with *value* which copies compound terms from the Heap to the global area. Again, it is the programmer/compiler's responsibility to ensure this copying does not unintentionally destroy another allocated global variable.

access(loc, value)

where *loc* dereferences to an integer constant corresponding to the word address within the global area of the variable to be accessed.

and   *value* typically dereferences to an unbound variable into which the value is to be placed.

access attempts to unify the values at *loc* and *value*. Again a special unify operation is used which copies compound terms from the global area to the top of the Heap.

There are several disadvantages to implementing global variables in this manner, the foremost being the forcing of global area allocation responsibility onto the programmer/compiler, where only static decisions are possible. This is primarily a problem when structures and lists are involved. Another disadvantage is that the global area, by its nature, is an area of the Data Space that is precluded from use by the dynamic storage allocation scheme of the PLM in general.

The primary advantage of this implementation is one of performance. Since *set* and *access* use only Data Space information, they may be realized and optimized for the existing Prolog functional unit facilities. As will be seen in Chapter 5, this is much more efficient than an operation performed by an outside functional unit.

General assert and retract - Overview. The mechanism described above does not have sufficient power to support general *assert* and *retract*. Thus some more general means of data base hacking must also be provided.

It has been observed in the folklore by both Prolog implementors and users that data base hacking can wreak havoc on performance of existing Prolog systems, and the implementation presented here is no exception.

It has been suggested [8] that the solution to this problem is to compile the invoking clausal form and perform a unification of this compiled code and the compiled code in the database. There are several problems with this approach for the PLM. The first concerns the representation of code in the Code Space (It should be noted that "compiling" the invoking form above means both compilation and assembly since the assembled form is the only one present in the Code Space). The unification algorithm in the PLM works on tagged 32 bit data items where the Code Space is a collection of opcodes and operands stored as untagged bytes. Conversion to tagged data item form and subsequent unification is an expensive operation due to its complexity and the fact that the conversion would most likely be done by the host processor.

A second, more serious objection to unifying compiled code stems from the optimizing efforts of the clause compiler where it comes to variable allocation. The allocation of variables to specific X or Y registers is a function of the entire clause. For example, consider the clause

$a(X,Y,Z) :- b(X,Y),c(Y,Z),d(Z),e(Z).$

as one of the clauses of procedure "a". The compiler will see the variables Y and Z as permanent variables with Y having the shorter lifetime. As a result Y will be assigned to register Y2 and Z to Y1 to facilitate environment trimming. The code for this clause is shown in Figure 3.18a. Now consider the retract goal

?- retract('a(X,Y,Z) :- W').

which through backtracking will ultimately remove all of the clauses of "a" from the database. In compiling the argument of retract (see Figure 3.18b) the compiler sees all variables as void variables and generates no code to handle them. The unification of these forms could not succeed.

An alternative solution proposed here is to maintain an indexed representation of the Prolog source amenable to the

---

```
    allocate
    get_variable  Y2,X2              %  b(X,
    get_variable  Y1,X3              %      Y),
    call  b/2,2
    put_unsafe_value  Y2,X1                 %  c(Y,
    put_value  Y1,X2                 %      Z),
    call  c/2,1
    put_value  Y1,X1              %  d(Z),
    call  d/1,1
    put_unsafe_value  Y1,X1                 %  e(Z).
    deallocate
    execute  e/1
```

a. Clause Code

```
_268:
    put_variable  X1,X1
    escape  retract/1
    proceed
```

b. Incorrect Query Code

Figure 3.18: A Problem Unifying Compiled Code.

---

unification algorithm of the PLM. The solution involves operations performed at compile time and link/load time as well as some host support for some of the builtins.

Before looking at the details of this method consider the structure representation of the clause

a(X,Y) :- b(X,Z),c(Y,Z).

shown in Figure 3.19 a,b. The structure ':-'/2 has 2 elements, the head and body of the clause. The head is the structure corresponding to the predicate a/2 and its arguments, the variables X and Y. The body of the clause is a nested structure with the primary functor ','/2 and elements as structures representing the subgoals of the clause. (The second element of ','/2 may itself be a ','/2 structure for clauses with more than 2 subgoals). As stated in Clocksin and Mellish [13], facts are considered to be clauses with a single subgoal, true, which always succeeds.

':-'(a(X,Y), ','(b(X,Z),c(Y,Z)))

a. Structure Representation

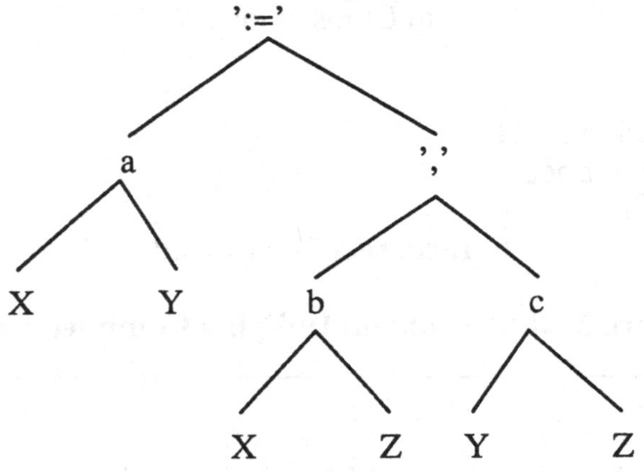

b. Tree Representation

Figure 3.19: Structure Representation of a Clause.

To provide the ability to unify with the structures described above at run time, the linker/loader must provide two library procedures (in compiled form) at load time. These are the predicates prolog_db/2 and prolog_db_body/4 shown in Figure 3.20. For a discussion of how these library routines work assume that prolog_db is invoked with a sufficiently instantiated clausal structure to identify a clause or clauses in the database as its first argument and an unbound variable as its second. (Sufficiently instantiated means that the predicate of the clause must be identified). The prolog_db procedure unifies the structure of the clause being sought binding Head to the head and Body to the body of the clause. The value of Index returned by prolog_db is an internal index of the clause found to unify. (These indices are assigned and maintained by the compiler and linker). Prolog_db has two subgoals, prolog_db_head/3 and prolog_db_body/4. Prolog_db_head finds a clause head in the database which unifies with the head and binds Index to its internal index and Vars to a list of variables appearing in the clause. (Note: with Head as the

---

```
prolog_db((Head :- Body),Index) :- prolog_db_head(Head,Index,Vars),
                        prolog_db_body(Head,Index,0,Vars).

prolog_db_body(X,Index,N,Vars) :- prolog _db_subgoal(Index,X,N,Vars).
prolog_db_body(true,Index,N,Vars) :- prolog_db_subgoal(Index,true,N,Vars).
prolog_db_body((X,Y),Index,N,Vars) :- prolog_db_subgoal(Index,X,N,Vars),
                        M is N + 1,
                        prolog_db_body(Index,Y,M,Vars).
```

Figure 3.20: Prolog Database Procedures.

---

first argument of prolog_db_head the compiled form of this procedure can make use of the indexing provided by the PLM). The
four arguments of prolog_db_body represent the body being
sought, the clause index identified by prolog_db_head, the subgoal
number being sought (0 initially), and the list of variables in the
clause. This list of variables assures that variables appearing in the
head correspond to those of the same name in the body. It is
necessary since the head and body of a clause are represented in
separate clauses in the database. The three clauses of the
prolog_db_body procedure perform a recursive search for each
subgoal in the clause in the prolog_db_subgoal database using the
subgoal index to ensure proper order and terminating with the last
subgoal true or simply a non-nested "," structure.

The procedures prolog_db_head prolog_db_subgoal are databases of facts representing all clause heads and body literals
(subgoals) in the program. These facts are added to the code by
the compiler while the source code is present. The database
entries for the familiar concat/3 procedure are shown in Figure
3.21. (Note: in compiled form the prolog_db_subgoal procedure
may be indexed by the Index argument).

---

prolog_db_head(concat([],L,L),0,[L]).
prolog_db_head(concat([X|L1],L2,[X|L3]),1,[X,L1,L2,L3]).

prolog_db_subgoal(0,true,0,[L]).
prolog_db_subgoal(1,concat(L1,L2,L3),0,[X,L1,L2,L3]).

Figure 3.21: Source database for concat

With these library procedures and source code databases in place, the task of implementing several of the more difficult predicates becomes straightforward. A few examples are shown in Figure 3.22. The built-in clause uses prolog_db directly. For retract, prolog_db is used to find the index of the clause to retract and then uses the external built-in retract_clause to remove it from the code. The details of retract clause will be discussed after the implementation of assert is described below.

Code Space Modification. The actual insertion of additional code into the Code Space by the assert family of built-ins is complicated by the fact that normal procedure compilation uses an intricate indexing scheme among the clauses of the procedure. Including the asserted clauses in the indexing scheme can be an expensive operation. As a result, three methods of adding clauses to a procedure are discussed here. It should be noted at the outset that the operation to add clause code to a procedure must be mirrored by updates to the prolog_db_head and prolog_db_subgoal databases. The details of this update are not provided here but the effect is to add clauses to the procedures implementing these databases and

---

clause(X,Y) :- prolog_db((X :- Y), _).

retract(X) :-   prolog_db(X,Index),
                 retract_clause(Index).

Figure 3.22: Example builtin code.

---

the methods described below can be used there as well.

The first and most expensive method is to pay the penalty for adding the new clause with full indexing. This involves first running the clause compiler on the new clause. With this code (in assembled form) and sufficient information on the clauses already present, such as the type and possibly value of the first parameter and the location of the code, the procedure compiler phase is run again to establish the new indexing scheme. Finally some loader operations must be performed to place the new clause code and modified indexing code into the code space. The clause compilation and procedure compilation phases, being written in Prolog may be run on the PLM (with some assistance from external builtins), however the load phase must be performed by the host. The code resulting from this method is indistinguishable from code generated as if the asserted clause had been present at the initial compilation. As a result, the run time efficiency of the procedure is at its maximum but the execution of the assert operation is expensive. This method of clause assertion is best suited for clauses which expect to be long lived, i.e. are not expected to be subsequently retracted, for example in adding newly generated theorems to a database in a theorem proving application.

The second method again involves using the clause compiler to compile the added clause and then simply linking it into the procedure code without regard to indexing. Two separate cases for asserta and assertz are considered. The operation *asserta* adds clauses at the beginning of the linearly searched list of clauses to try.

In order for *asserta* to add clauses to an existing procedure, the original code must have been compiled with the appropriate hooks. Since the entry point of the procedure may have been compiled into arbitrary locations in other procedures, it must remain fixed. This can be accomplished via an **indirect call** mechanism realized by an **execute** instruction at the fixed entry point which in effect jumps to the procedure code. The first instruction of the original compiled code must be padded by **nop** instructions to reserve Code Space for future code modifications. This procedure configuration can be seen in Block 1 of Figure 3.23. Here, procedure "a" entry point contains an **execute** instruction indicating the code at location *ra*. Block 2 shows what happens after clause compilation when a new clause, *na1*, is asserted by asserta. The instructions in *italics* are those that have been modified. The *asserta* function modifies the address at the entry point to jump to the new clause. The new clause begins with a **try_me_else** instruction who's argument is set as the address originally at the entry point. This sets up a choice point for the added layer of indexing. Finally, the **nop** instructions in the original code are replaced by a **trust_me_else fail** instruction to remove the added choice point.

Block 3 shows the results of subsequently asserting a clause *na2*. Again, the entry point is modified and the **try_me_else** instruction is placed in *na2*. Finally, in this case, the **try_me_else** instruction in *na1* is changed to a **retry_me_else** instruction to modify the choice point now set up by *na2*. Block 4 shows the results of asserting *na3*. Note that in each instance, as a new clause is asserted, only three easily identified Code Space locations need to be modified.

The assertz builtin adds clauses at the end of the a procedure. As with *asserta*, *assertz* requires compiled in "hooks" in the original code. Block 1 of Figure 3.24 shows these hooks. An appropriate number of **nop** instructions is included in the original code, and the entry point has an additional field following the **execute** instruction which is never executed but merely contains the address of the current last clause of the procedure.

Block 2 shows the results of asserting a new clause, *na1* by assertz. The **nop** instructions in *ra* are replaced by a **try_me_else** instruction indicating the new code, the new code is prefaced by a **trust_me_else fail** instruction, and finally, the last clause address in the entry point is updated. Block 3 shows the results of a

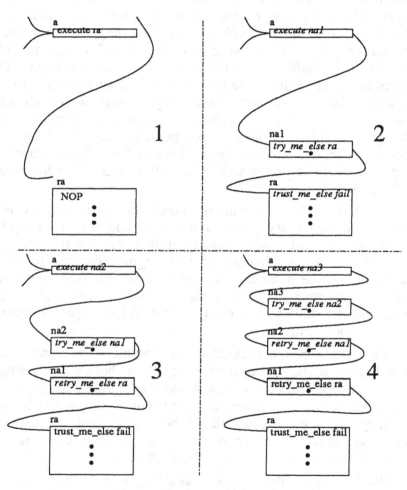

Figure 3.23: Using Asserta

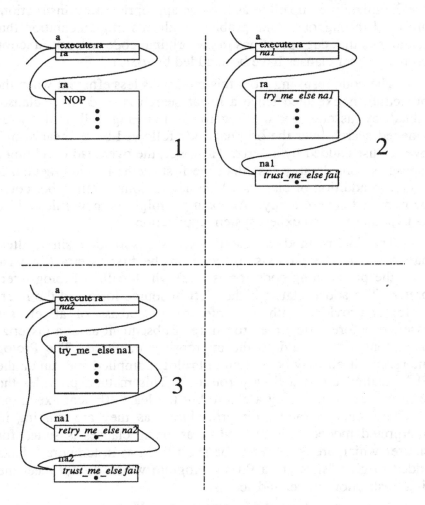

Figure 3.24: Using Assertz.

subsequent *assertz*. Note that the operations of *asserta* and *assertz* are completely compatible as long as appropriate **nop** instructions are used throughout. One problem with this implementation that remains is that **cut** operations in the original code will not function correctly after clauses have been added by *assertz*.

The code resulting from this method is less efficient when the procedure is executed since a linear search is made over clauses added by asserta without regard to indexing followed by an indexed search over the original code followed by a linear search over clauses added by assertz. However, the overhead of adding a clause is considerably less than the first method. This method is suited to addition of clauses which have a long lifetime but could be retracted subsequently. An example might be new rules added as hypotheses in an expert system application.

The final method for asserting clauses is to add a single alternative before the pre-existing code on the first asserta (likewise after the pre-existing code for assertz) which calls a Prolog interpreter. The added clause is then left in source form and the interpreter is provided with a pointer to a database of all clauses asserted before (after) the procedure. Subsequent asserta (assertz) operations simply add to the appropriate database. The Prolog interpreter itself may be written in Prolog, compiled and run on the PLM (called up as a library routine). This method provides the least overhead in adding a clause but the least efficient execution of added clauses (and their procedures) as they are running in interpreted mode. This method of asserting clauses is suited for clauses which are expected to be short lived as in temporary facts added to give "state" to a Prolog program which do not meet the rigid restrictions of set and access.

Having described the methods of adding clauses to a procedure by assert, the actions of retract_clause should be obvious. To retract an asserted clause added by the interpreter method simply involves removing it from the appropriate database. For a clause added by the compile and link method, the appropriate **try**, retry, and **trust** instructions must be modified to snip out the clause from the procedure. To retract a clause added by the compile and index method or to retract a clause from the original compilation, the snipping operation may be required in more than one link chain as well as modification of hash tables to completely remove a clause from any indexing scheme. In all cases, appropriate code modification may be needed to cover the boundary condition of "last clause of this method" removal.

CHAPTER SUMMARY

This Chapter has suggested several modifications and additions to the WAM to provide a specification for a Prolog Machine called the PLM. Formats for code and data representation were provided. A cdr-coded representation of compound terms was proposed and an additional instruction was added to the instruction set to support it. Several of the features omitted from the WAM such as the *cut* operation and built-in predicates were addressed and the alternatives discussed. A modified form of backtracking, termed sidetracking, was introduced and shown to be effective in improving the performance of tail recursive predicates as well as reducing repetition of work in head unification for some forms of procedures. Finally, several approaches to implementing the *assert* and *retract* built-ins of Prolog for compiled code were discussed.

CHAPTER 4

THE ARCHITECTURE BECOMES A MACHINE

IMPLEMENTING THE PLM

The previous Chapter provided the specification for the Instruction Set Architecture (ISA) of the PLM. This Chapter realizes the ISA by defining the microarchitecture of the PLM and describing the physical hardware which implements that microarchitecture. The next Chapter discusses and analyses the projected performance.

In defining the microarchitecture for a computing system, the boundary of the system being described and the specification of the interface must be provided. For the discussions in this Chapter, the boundaries of the PLM enclose the datapath and microengine of the processor, and the buffers, caches and Prefetch Unit which make up the PMI (see Figure 3.1). Since the PLM is designed as a coprocessor to a host system, the interface to the host assumed for these discussions is a 32 bit Processor/Memory (PM) bus. The PLM is a memory mapped device on the bus. The host system is assumed to provide the memory subsystem including all memory management functions for the virtual address space of the PLM as well as processor support for I/O, Floating Point and other non-logical operations, and front panel control for the PLM. In particular, the hardware implementation of the PLM is designed around an NCR/32 system [2].

The organization of this Chapter begins with a discussion of the instruction fetching operation provided by the Prefetch Unit and then describes the data path and microengine separately. Next the integration and tuning of the data path and microengine are described. Finally, a discussion of the path to memory, particularly the Data Space, provides the motivation for the implementation of the various caches and buffers provided by the PLM. Some of the numeric performance results mentioned in this Chapter were obtained from the simulators running benchmark programs. The simulators themselves as well as more detailed results are discussed in Chapter 5.

THE PREFETCH UNIT

In any processor design, two operations which must be performed for each instruction are fetching and decoding. One way to improve processor performance is to overlap these operations with execution of a previous instruction. In the PLM, since memory access time is long relative to processor cycle time, instructions are continually fetched in advance, partially decoded, and stored in an Instruction Buffer until requested by the processor to be executed. This section describes these operations.

The Prefetch Unit is responsible for fetching instructions from memory, partially decoding the instructions, aligning them to conform to one of two instruction formats expected by the processor and storing them in the Instruction Buffer. As such, the P register or Program pointer of the PLM is maintained entirely in the Prefetch Unit. Instruction prefetching is made simple in the PLM due to the fact that the instruction set includes only simple change of control flow instructions. These instructions are:

call	proceed
execute	switch_on_term
try	switch_on _constant
retry	switch_on_structure
trust	fail

The Prefetch Unit continually requests instruction fetch memory accesses from the memory interface. These requests are serviced when all higher priority memory requests have been serviced. For non-branch instructions, the P register is appropriately incremented from information in the size field of the opcode, and a new request is issued. For some of the branch instructions, namely those in the left column above, the jump address is present as the first operand of the instruction. The Prefetch Unit can simply reload the P register from this operand and continue to prefetch instructions. One complication arises for these simple control flow change instructions in that when they are executed, these instructions usually need the value of the P register to save it as part of the machine state (the **execute** instruction is the only exception). However, since the Prefetch Unit has continued prefetching, the value of the P register is incorrect and in general unpredictable by the time the instruction is executed. Therefore, the Prefetch Unit must recognize these instructions and save the value of the P register in place of the first operand in the Instruction Buffer. Thus when the instruction is finally executed, argument 1 will contain the value of the P register needed. These instructions are identified by the S bit in the opcode.

Those branch instructions in the right column above, however, determine the branch address based on conditions that exist when the instruction is executed. These instructions are called *jump* instructions and have the jump bit (J) set in the opcode. When the Prefetch unit encounters a jump instruction, it suspends further prefetch requests until the jump instruction is executed and the P register is reloaded by the processor. In these instances, the Instruction Buffer is allowed to empty, thus causing the processor to wait for the next instruction to be fetched once the new P value has been determined. One method for improving performance in this area is to do branch prediction and continue prefetching instructions. When the jump instruction is finally executed, if the prediction was correct, then no stall is required by the processor. If the prediction was not correct, then the instructions in the buffer are invalid and the processor must wait for the proper next instruction to be fetched. However, this stall is no longer than that if no prediction had been made. Thus the performance gain is related the the ability to correctly predict the branch address relatively often; but performance is never degraded by branch prediction.

In studying the feasibility of branch prediction for the PLM jump instructions, several features are evident. First, due to the source of the branch address for the **proceed, switch_on_constant,** and **switch-on_structure** instructions (the CP register or an address obtained from a hash table), the ability to predict the branch address is not very good. For **switch_on_term** however, there are only four possible branch addresses included as offsets in the instruction itself. A default condition for proceeding to the next instruction makes the choice for a simple prediction scheme obvious, namely continue prefetching as if no jump had occurred. In the current instruction set, the default condition for the **switch_on_term** instruction is an unbound variable in AX1. Simulation results show that for the benchmark programs, this branch is taken only 7% of the time. Thus branch prediction would not realize much performance gain. However; the same simulation results show that for the benchmark programs, the branch for list type values in AX1 occurs 63% of the time. Branch prediction is one area for future enhancement of the PLM, however it is not incorporated in the current design.

A second function of the Prefetch Unit is to begin the decode of the instruction. This partial decode is realized as an instruction alignment and separation of arguments. As instructions are fetched, they are divided into three sections before being saved in the Instruction Buffer (see Figure 3.8b). The three sections are:

1. opcode -   A single byte containing the opcode.

2. Arg1 -   32 bits containing the first operand. For
                  instructions with only a single byte ar-
                  gument 1, the byte is right justified. For
                  instructions with no operands, a dummy
                  Arg1 section is buffered.

3. Args2/3-   32 bits containing second and third
                  operands. This section is only buffered
                  for instructions which have more than
                  one argument. Since arguments 2 and 3
                  are always single bytes, only 2 bytes of
                  the 32 bit word of Args2/3 are utilized.

The Instruction Buffer is physically realized as two buffers; a byte
wide opcode buffer with one entry per instruction, and a 32 bit
wide argument buffer with one or two entries per instruction. In
the PLM hardware, these buffers were implemented using RAMS
and two counters to provided the FIFO operation required. The
processor fetches instructions from the buffer in two stages. In
stage 1, an opcode and an Arg1 entry are fetched simultaneously.
The optional stage 2 fetches the Args2/3 entry if required.

One final feature of the Prefetch Unit is the ability to handle a
fail operation detected by the processor. When an instruction in
execution causes a **fail**, all instructions in the buffer are no longer
valid. Thus the Prefetch Unit must invalidate the Instruction
Buffer and wait for the P register to be reloaded at which time it
requests an instruction fetch operation from the memory interface.
Since the processor cannot continue past the **fail** operation until
the new instruction is fetched, the memory request has the highest
priority. A processor stall is further precluded by having the **fail**
operation reload the P register early in its microsequence so that
the instruction fetch and partial decode can occur in parallel with
with the remaining state restoring operation of **fail**.

In summary, the Prefetch Unit continually fetches instructions from memory, aligns the instruction fields into two or three sections, and buffers the sections for the processor. The processor takes the instruction sections in one or two stages. Instruction fetch memory requests are serviced at a priority below data reads and writes unless the instruction buffer becomes empty or a **fail** operation occurs (forcing the buffer to become empty), when instruction fetch becomes the highest priority. Prefetch continues as bus traffic permits until either the buffer is full or a jump instruction is encountered. This scheme for prefetching minimizes the processor wait time for instruction fetching. The Prefetch Unit hardware for the PLM was built and tested and is described in Williams [65].

DEFINING A BASIC DATA PATH

The muscle of the PLM consists of the registers, busses, and functional units making up the data path shown in Figure 4.1. The general form of the data path is based on a Prolog processor description by Warren and Tick [57]. Modifications to this design were strongly influenced by the form of the microcode. In fact, the data path and the microcode evolved in parallel, with each exerting influence on the form of the other. An additional driving force behind some design decisions was the space availability on the boards used for the current implementation.

The overall operation of the Prolog engine can be viewed as taking place in three stages; an Access stage where pertinent data is retrieved from processor registers; an Execute stage where the appropriate operation is performed; and a Put-away stage where results are returned to the processor registers. The three stage flow is reflected in the bussing structure. Four major busses are provided, grouped in two pairs separated by registers. These bus pairs represent the Access and Put-away stages. The Execute stage is realized in the ALU and the special paths associated with the MAR and MDR registers. Every attempt is made in the microcode to

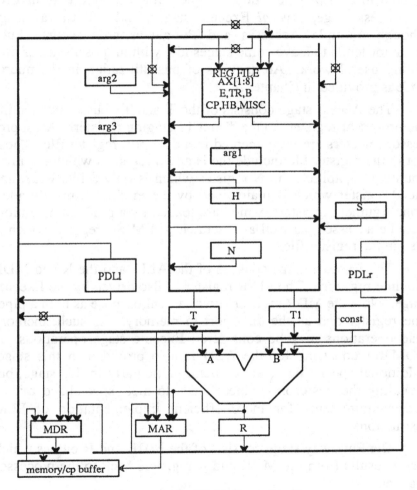

Figure 4.1: PLM Data Path.

statically pipeline the operations of the three stages within a micro-routine. Due the nature of the operations which must be performed in a PLM instruction, a typical microroutine may involve an Access stage, *several* Execute stages, and a Put-away stage (though multiple Accesses and Put-aways also occur). Such behavior tends to leave some stages idle without possibility of providing useful work. An analysis of bus utilization in the microcode is provided in Chapter 5.

The Access stage consists of the **T** and **T1** busses connecting the processor registers to the T and T1 staging registers. Most processor registers are implemented in a dual port register file. Those not in the register file include the H and S registers which require a counting capability, the N register which is only 8 bits wide, and the P register which is maintained by the Prefetch Unit. In addition, argument registers, which are loaded by a prefetch operation, may be accessed, as well as a scratch pad MISC register which is also in the register file.

The Execute stage consists of the ALU, and the R and MDR pipeline registers. The MAR register is also driven by the Execute stage. Note the MDR register serves a dual purpose as both a pipeline register and as the data port to memory. As such, memory read operations may be considered Execute stage operations. A ROM for constants for the ALU is also provided in this stage. Additional special paths are evident, particularly in this stage, but including the bus cross-connect links, to meet specialized microcode requirements for more efficient implementation of PLM instructions.

The Put-away stage consists of the **MDR** and **R** busses which direct results from the MDR and R registers back to the processor registers.

Finally, the PDL area of the Data Space is actually implemented entirely within the processor. Since a PDL entry consists of two 32 bit items, two RAMS called *PDLl* and *PDLr* are provided. Not shown in the figure is the counter register for maintaining the address pointer into the PDL.

DEFINING A MICROENGINE

The heart of the PLM is a microsequencing engine with a wide (134 bit) horizontal microword. The primary function of this engine is to dispatch signals to control the data paths throughout the machine, as well as to provide control signals for its own internal paths. In addition, the microengine must support an interface between the PLM and the host processor for both control (start, stop, reset, etc.) and status reporting (display state, goal failure, etc.). This section describes the design of the microengine.

The operation of this or any microengine is basically a two-stroke cycle:

1) Dispatch data path control signals.

2) Calculate the address and fetch the next microinstruction.

Since these two operations are relatively independent, (or they may be made so by a delayed branch mechanism), they may be done in parallel. The PLM microengine is shown in Figure 4.2. It consists of a microstore (1K words) and logic for determining the address of the next microinstruction. The basic PLM cycle begins by latching the microword into the microinstruction register. The output of this register provides the control signals to the execution engine as well as inputs to the next state logic.

The next state logic takes the current microinstruction information, which includes a 10 bit field containing a next state address seed, as well as other control bits, and processor status information (condition codes, mode bit, tag bits, etc.) to produce the next instruction address which is presented to the microstore for look-up in time to be available for the beginning of the next cycle. The next instruction address is derived in several stages involving various decisions which will be traced from the address

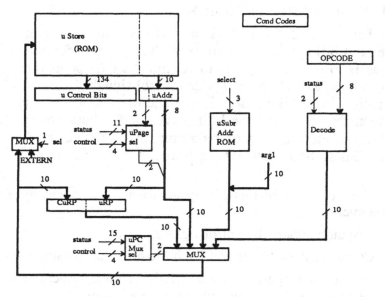

Figure 4.2: MicroEngine.

input to the microstore backwards through the logic.

The first decision is based on whether the next address source will be internal or external. The external address source is provided to allow the host processor to force a branch to any location in the microstore. In general, control operations are initiated by the host processor by writing a control word into a specific word in its address space (for the NCR, a word in scratch pad memory is chosen for ease of decoding). The microengine recognizes when this location is written, latches the data from the bus, and initiates the appropriate control action. Control operations can be divided into two groups, forced microbranch operations and processor state change operations.

Forced microbranch operations are identified by a bit in the control word, called the interrupt bit, and utilize a 10 bit field of the control word as the target next microaddress. When an interrupt occurs, the desired effect is for microsequencing to continue at the target address with the control return register frozen holding the address of the next microinstruction to be executed when normal microsequencing resumes. In order for this to be true, the input to the control return register must come from the next microaddress lines, not the next microaddress seed as is the case for the return register.

In general, a forced microbranch can occur to any address in the microstore; however, certain precautions must be observed by the executing microcode. First, in order to resume normal sequencing, the last instruction of the control microroutine must include control bits to gate the control return register to the return inputs of the uPC mux and to direct the uPC Mux Select Logic to perform the return. As a side effect of this return, the control return register should be enabled to latch on every clock once again. In addition, operations performed within a control initiated microsequence should not affect any processor status information as the branch status of the microsequence interrupted is not known (i.e. the normal microsequence may be about to branch based on processor status when interrupted). Typical control initiated microroutines include:

1) RESET - A microsequence which clears/initializes all processor registers including the P register to a "reset" condition. The sequence terminates with an instruction fetch.

2) DISPLAY REGISTERS - a microsequence which dumps all internal processor registers to a specific area of the Data Space via the normal memory interface. The sequence terminates with a wait followed by a control return operation. The display microroutine may also restore processor registers before return.

The interrupt capability provided by the mechanism described above is not as general as that for a general purpose processor. However, it does provide sufficient functionality to control the PLM as a loosely-coupled coprocessor from a general purpose host. The interrupt mechanism provided is also useful for debugging the hardware during testing.

The second group of control operations, processor state change operations, are each identified by a bit in the control word. These operations are not directly supported by the fields of the microword. They include:

1)   CONTINUE - to awaken the processor from a wait state and continue normal microsequencing operations.

2)   SINGLE INSTRUCTION - sets a control bit which causes the Instruction Decode Logic to force a wait on the next instruction boundary.

3)   SINGLE CLOCK - executes a single microinstruction and puts the processor in a wait state.

Continuing to trace the generation on next microaddress, the next decision is to select one of four possible internal sources for the next microaddress. This branch decision is known as M-branching. These sources are:

1)   Instruction Decode Logic (I Port).

2)   Fundamental Operation Select (S Port).

3)   microReturn Register (R Port).

4)   microAddress Seed (P Port).

Each of these sources will be discussed in turn, but first the basis of the choice is described.

The selection of one internal source is made via a multiplexor and determined by the uPC Mux Select Logic. This logic takes five bits of control from the microinstruction representing a branch code, and 19 bits of status information as input to produce the 2 bits of select output to select the multiplexors. To allow sufficient time in a microcycle for all decisions to be made and an access to the microstore accomplished, all status information must be valid at the beginning of the cycle.

In the microcode, a delayed branch feature was added for those branch conditions which rely on results of operations in the data path (ALU operations and PDL operations). Since these results take time to produce, they must be produced on the cycle before the branch and latched into a condition code register. The branch is delayed until the next cycle and is made based on the values in the condition code register.

The output of the instruction decode logic is selected as the next microinstruction address whenever an instruction boundary is encountered in the microcode, referred to as an *IFETCH* call, i.e. whenever execution of a new PLM instruction is begun. This logic is responsible for determining the appropriate microroutine entry point based on the opcode and some status information.

The opcode is provided by the OPCODE register in the microengine. The opcode register is loaded during instruction pre-fetching from the Prefetch Unit. Prefetching, as described in the last section, takes place in two phases. To prevent prefetch from slowing down the processor (adding extra states to do instruction fetch), the microcode is written to perform phase 1 and, if possible, phase 2 prefetch in parallel with the execution of the previous instruction. Phase 1 prefetch may be done anytime after the last use of arg1 in a microroutine by issuing a prefetch1 request to the Prefetch Unit. The OPCODE register is implemented as a transparent latch so that a phase 1 prefetch and an *IFETCH* call can be done in the same cycle. Phase 2 prefetch may be done anytime after phase 1 and after the last use of arg2 and arg3 in a microroutine. The OPCODE register is also used to determine if a phase 2 prefetch is required. This operation is described in the next section.

The mode bit also contributes to the decode logic. The mode bit is set by several PLM instructions to specify whether processing of a list or structure is to proceed in read or write mode. It is used by the unify instructions, some of which have different microroutine entry points based on mode.

The fundamental operation select logic is used when the sequence of microstates is to branch to a microroutine entry point due to other than an *IFETCH* call. This occurs most frequently in the microcode for invocation of fundamental operations. Three bits of control are provided from the current microinstruction to select the entry point from a ROM.

The microengine also has the facility for performing micro-call and return operations. This facility is needed to support the **dereference, decdr** and **trail** operations in the microcode. Results of these operations require further processing by the microroutine calling **dereference** or **decdr** so some facility for returning is needed. The **trail** microroutine either returns to the **unify** micro-routine or performs an *IFETCH* call upon completion. The micro-routines for other fundamental operations could be arranged so that they terminated in an *IFETCH* call and therefore require no return. To realize this mechanism, a microreturn register is provided which latches the next address from the microword under control of the current microinstruction when a microcall is to occur. (In fact, the call to dereference is always conditional with the decision made by the uPC MUX Select Logic). A microreturn, then, is per-formed by selecting the microreturn register as the source of the next microinstruction address. Only a single microreturn register is provided, for this purpose, so only one level of call may be per-formed. A second microreturn register is provided for use by the host processor as described previously.

Every microinstruction contains a 10 bit field called the next microaddress seed. For normal, non-branching, sequences, this seed is selected as the next microaddress. The M-branching described above provides one mechanism for microbranching, however, this mechanism is not sufficiently powerful to support all types of branches in the microcode. In particular, while most branches are two-way, some three-way and four-way branches occur. To support this, 2 bits of the microaddress seed are considered to be page bits and may be modified by the the microPage Select Logic. Under this scheme, the microstore is viewed as divided into 4 pages of 256 words. A four-way branch is realized as a branch to the same address on the appropriate page. Two-way and three-way branches may also be done through this mechanism. This form of branching is known as P-branching.

The microPage Select Logic takes the seed page bits, four control bits as inputs and 9 bits of processor status information, and produces the two page bits as output.

In addition to providing four-way branch capability, the microPage Select mechanism helps reduce the logic required to realize microbranching entirely. Without such a capability, the complexity of the uPC Mux Select Logic would have increased somewhat, but the Fundamental Operation Select Logic and/or the Instruction Decode Logic would have to greatly expand to accommodate all of the target branch addresses.

The **escape** instruction presents a special case to the microengine. This instruction is used to invoke a Prolog built-in function specified by its 32 bit argument 1. The microroutine for the **escape** instruction must branch to the appropriate microsequence to process the built-in. This is done by gating the 10 least significant bits of arg1 to the S Port of the uPC Mux and selecting these inputs as the next microaddress. Thus, microcoded internal built-in functions are uniquely specified by the 10 bits of microaddress of their entry point. All of the externally implemented built-in functions have the same 10 least significant bits to branch to the same entry point, and are uniquely identified by the remaining bits of arg1 to the host.

The microsequence entered for external built-in functions dumps a number of AX registers (corresponding to the arity of the built-in), the arg1 register specifying the built-in and the H, B, HB, and TR registers to a specific location in the Data Space (a communication page), signals the host processor, and places the PLM into a wait state suspending microsequencing. Upon completion of the built-in operation, the host processor signals the PLM and the microengine resumes processing the external built-in microsequence. This sequence then possibly reloads the H and TR registers from the host processor memory (to capture any results of heap or trail additions) and terminates normally with an *IFETCH* call.

The wait state of the PLM is initiated by a bit in the microword and causes the microengine to suspend all sequencing. In the wait state, the status of the microengine is frozen to allow resumption of sequencing as if no wait had occurred. This is implemented by inhibiting the load of the microinstruction register. The microengine is awaken from a wait state by a continue signal from the host processor.

Besides determining next state, the microword contains fields for controlling the processor data path.

TUNING THE DATA PATH AND THE MICROCODE

As the PLM evolved several additional features were added to the data path to enhance performance. These modifications concern support for data tagging and microbranch decisions based on tags.

The first such feature concerns the tags of the AX registers. A common operation at the beginning of many data manipulation instructions, particularly the get and unify instructions, is to dereference the operand specified in the instruction. Dereferencing involves a microsubroutine call to the dereference routine if the operand is a variable. To eliminate extra states involved in this call a conditional call mechanism is provided in the microengine. The page modified microaddress seed is latched in the uRP register and also provided to the P port of the uPC Mux. The uPC Mux select logic then decides to make the call (select S) or not (select

P) based on the tag of the operand. Since these operands are found in AX registers, quick access is required to the tag bits of the registers. However, the AX registers are stored in a register file and the access time to the tags is too long to allow microbranching in the same cycle. To alleviate this timing constraint the tag bits of the AX registers are shadowed in PALS so that all 8 tag bit pairs are available in parallel. An 8-way multiplexor is then provided to select tags for either AX[0], AX[arg1], AX[arg2], or AX[RAS] where arg1 and arg2 are from the argument registers holding the arguments of the instruction and RAS is a microword field specifying an AX register. The circuit for this is shown schematically in Figure 4.3. Thus for the frequent operation of dereferencing operands the tag shadow and microbranch logic provide an essentially free mechanism for microsubroutine call (i.e. no extra states).

In addition to the ability to branch in microcode based on tags from a variety of sources, a tagged architecture must provide the ability to construct new tagged data items. In the PLM this ability is provided in the MDR register. The MDR consists of three different fields; a two bit primary tag field, a one bit cdr field, and a 29 bit value field (including the garbage collect bit). Each field has independent sources under microcode control. The tag and cdr fields are loaded together but independently from the value filed. This is shown in Figure 4.4. The sources for the tag field are:

> T tags
> T1 tags
> microword MDTGS field
> Same source as the value field

The sources for the cdr field are:

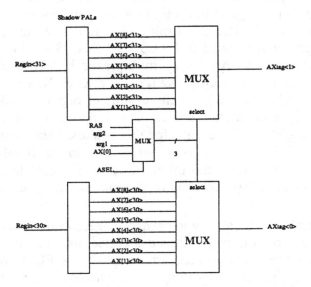

Figure 4.3: Selecting Tags for Branching.

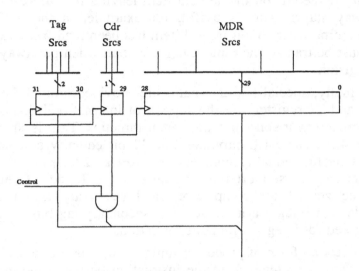

Figure 4.4: MDR Register.

T cdr bit
cut flag
R cdr bit
Explicit 1 or 0
current MDR cdr bit

(This last source allows the tag field to be loaded while retaining the current cdr field value). The source to the MDR cdr field is generated by a PAL in the hardware.

This configuration allows a very flexible construction of tagged data items. For example, a data item could be constructed with the value field of the T register, the cdr bit of the R register, and forced variable primary tags.

One last tag support feature of the MDR register is the ability to turn off the cdr bit of the data item leaving the MDR during a Put-away stage. This is useful, for example, in the unify_cdr microroutine where a cdr tagged item has been read from memory and must be transformed into a non-cdr item when put away in an AX register.

Finally, special tag data paths are provided around the ALU and T and T1 registers for the support of internal built-ins involving term comparisons and integer arithmetic. This is shown in Figure 4.5. The ALU provides full 32 bit equality comparisons and 28 bit non-equality compares as well as 28 bit addition and subtraction. To support this, the tags of the T and T1 registers must be zeroed for comparisons and secondary tag bits sign extended for integer arithmetic. The secondary tag bits must also be restored for integer arithmetic operations.

A second form of processor tuning concerns the second stage of instruction prefetch from the instruction buffer in the Prefetch Unit to the microengine. As was described earlier, instructions come from the Prefetch Unit in one of two formats requiring one or two prefetch operations. All microroutines provide a phase 1 operation to get the opcode and arg1 from the Instruction Buffer. However, it is not always possible for a microroutine to do the phase 2 operation before beginning the next macroinstruction. For those microroutines that do a phase 2 prefetch the microengine, in conjunction with the instruction decode logic, decides whether the next macroinstruction needs arg2 or arg3 and issues a request to the I-buffer accordingly, otherwise the prefetch 2 microorder is ignored. If however, an IFETCH call is done to begin a macroinstruction that needs arg2 and/or arg3 and a phase 2 operation has not been done, the opcode decode logic selects an alternate entry point for the microroutine to perform the missing phase 2 prefetch. Thus the microengine has been optimized to allow a phase 2 prefetch to take place in parallel with other operations if time permits, but can insert an extra state when the previous instruction was not able to complete the phase 2 prefetch.

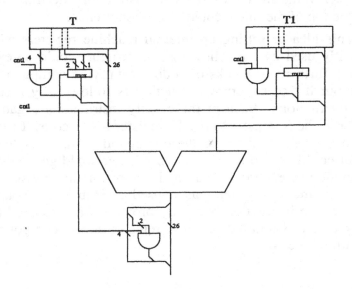

Figure 4.5: Tags in the ALU.

Once a working microcode implementation of the instruction set was completed, static analysis of the microcode revealed several areas where the microcode could be tuned to the available data paths.

A frequent operation noted in may microroutines was the calculation of Y register address in those instructions involving permanent variables. The first microstate of these instructions always contained a transfer of the E register to either the T or T1 register in preparation for the E + Yspec calculation. However, at instruction boundaries, T and T1 did not contain useful data. By imposing the protocol at instruction boundaries that the T register contain a copy of the value of the E register It was found that one microstate could be eliminated from most microroutines involving Y register calculations. By expanding this protocol to include the B register value in the T1 register, instructions needing to determine the top of the Stack could also be shortened.

This idea of setting up internal machine registers with data frequently used by the following microroutine could be extended one step further. In blocks of code for unifying compound data a get or put list or structure instruction is followed by a series of unify instructions. Each of these unify instructions began with a transfer of the S register to the T1 register followed by T1 to MAR to read the next element of the compound term. This two stage transfer could be shortened if the S register could get to the MAR in a single cycle. Rather than add a path for this transfer, it was noted that the R register was unused at instruction boundaries. Therefore the instruction boundary protocol was extended to have a copy of the S register in the R register during compound term unification blocks.

THE PATH TO MEMORY

As was stated in an earlier section, the memory access time provided by the host processor could cause serious performance degradations in the PLM, an example of the classic von Neumann bottleneck. A mechanism to circumvent the problem for accesses to the Code Space by prefetching instructions whenever possible has been discussed. This section will describe several mechanisms incorporated in the design to alleviate the memory bottleneck between the PLM and the Data Space. It should be mentioned here that many of the buffering schemes used suggested themselves upon examination of memory reference patterns observed in simulation runs of benchmark programs.

The first observation to be made is that memory references may be classified statically in the microcode based on the area of the Data Space being referenced. The five classes are:

1) References to the current Choice Point. These references are made to a fixed sized block on the Stack relative to the **B** register. With the single exception of popping a new choice point to be current, Choice Point references are often near the top of the Stack.

2) References to the current Environment. These references are made to a variable sized block on the Stack relative to the **E** register when referring to a permanent variable or one of the four state items included in the environment. Again, with the exception of restoring an old environment to be current, these references are often near the top of the Stack.

3) References to the Trail. These references are made in a true last-in first-out manner to a variable sized block in the Trail area of the Data Space.

4) References to the Heap. As the Heap is managed in only a pseudo-stack manner, Heap references relative to the **H** and particularly the **S** registers may be to arbitrary locations in the Heap.

5) Random references. These references may be either to arbitrary locations in the Heap or to deep locations on the Stack (as in a reference to a non-local permanent variable located in a previous environment). Due to the nature of the origin of these references (for example as the result of a dereference operation), it is not possible to statically identify the area referenced.

These five classes can be further subdivided as read and write references. The first mechanism considered is write buffering for all classes of references. This is described in the next section. Of the remaining reference types, random and Heap reads are too diffuse for simple buffering schemes. Some form of cache could be used to reduce the bottleneck delays for these references, however; due to space and complexity restrictions on this design, such schemes have not been further considered.

Write Buffering.

An idealized von Neumann memory interface would have memory access time match processor cycle time. Thus a memory reference could be done in one cycle and memory would appear no more distant than on board registers. Unfortunately, all too often this is not the case, particularly with a large main memory. One resolution for the discrepancy in time used by small systems is to lengthen the cycle time of the processor. This would produce an unacceptable performance degradation in this design since benchmark data indicates that on average, only one in three processor cycles includes a memory reference. The alternative is to insert wait states in the processor to wait for the completion of a memory access when needed. This is the tack adopted in this design, with a few exceptions.

The first exception concerns memory writes. Simulations show that on average 49.8% of all memory accesses are writes. Once a memory write is initiated, it is not necessary for the processor to wait to see its successful completion, so long as the data is eventually written, thus saving almost half of the wait states. To the processor, the ideal one cycle memory access can be apparently true for writes. However, since write requests can now occur faster then they can be serviced, it is possible for a backlog to develop. (In this design, this is particularly evident in the creation of a choice point where 15 write requests occur in 15 cycles). To handle the backlog, the memory interface includes a storage buffer to hold outstanding write requests. Memory writes are serviced by the host processor as time permits. Memory writes are given highest priority for service unless, as described in the previous section, the instruction buffer empties which means the PLM has no instruction ready for execution, i.e. nothing to do. Memory write priority is higher than memory read priority, since a read request could refer to a location with an outstanding write request. The simplest solution to this data consistency dilemma is to hold the read request (and therefore the PLM) until all write requests have been serviced. While this could easily cause unnecessary idling of the PLM, checking for the exceptional condition is not currently feasible based on available space in this design.

One additional safeguard is built in to the write buffer mechanism. Should the write buffer fill, the processor is held on a subsequent write request until space is available in the buffer. In the worst case, this results in performance as if there were no write buffer during the times when the write buffer is full.

Choice Point Cache.

The previous section has described a scheme for buffering all memory write operations to improve the effective access time. This section begins to look at buffering read operations. The technique used for writes will obviously not suffice for read since typically there is little else to do after a read request is issued before the data is required. The technique to be used here is to keep a local copy of parts of the memory within the processor. The first candidate for such an approach is the Choice Point.

As described previously, a choice point is a fixed sized block of memory which holds the state of the processor to be used when backtracking. At any given time only one existing choice point is likely to be accessed, namely the current Choice Point, i.e. the last one created. Access to previous choice points occurs only when one of these previous choice points is to become current, discarding all intervening state. The two forms of read access to choice points are localized to a few instances in the microcode; during a **fail** operation, where the Choice Point is read to restore state; and during one of the **trust** or **cut** instructions, where part of the Choice Point is accessed to find a previous choice point to make current. In addition, writes to a choice point are localized to two instances; during a **try** instruction, when a new choice point is created; and during a **retry** instruction, when part of the current choice Point is modified.

Several alternatives have been proposed for buffering choice point data including shadow registers [58] and a top of Stack cache [57]. The mechanism proposed for the PLM to cache the choice point is as follows. Data written to a choice point will also be written in the local cache. Since the choice point is fixed in size, the cache can be fixed in size (in this case, 16 words - the closest power of 2). Since only one choice point is considered current and is always accessed via an offset from the B register, access to the cache can be uniquely mapped via the least significant few bits of the absolute address in memory (in this case 4 bits). When a choice point has been written in the cache (and write requests issued and buffered to be written in memory), a processor status bit is set to indicate a valid choice point cache. When read access to the current choice point is attempted, if the choice point cache is marked as valid, the cache can immediately supply the requested data and the memory read request can be inhibited. If the choice point cache is marked as invalid, then a normal memory read request is issued. The choice point cache is marked invalid by one of the **trust** or **cut** instructions when the B register is reloaded. Rather then attempt to update the cache when it is invalidated, updating is delayed until the next **fail** operation since at that time the entire choice point is accessed. With the cache marked invalid, memory must service the choice point access, however; during that access, the cache may be reloaded as a side effect and then marked valid on the completion of the **fail** operation. Any subsequent access to the choice point, as long as it remains current, is serviced by the cache. This delayed update scheme ensures that no extra effort (and no time or memory bandwidth) is wasted validating the cache with a choice point that is discarded without being used.

The above scheme has been incorporated in the simulator and tested on the benchmark programs. The instrumentation data shows that an average of 46% of all memory reads are choice point reads, of which 87% are serviced by the buffer.

Environment and Trail Buffering.

A mechanism similar to the choice point cache may enhance the effective access times for references to the current environment and to the trail. There are several important differences which must be considered.

Like choice point references, access to the trail is localized in the microcode, in this case, to a single instance for read access, namely during the **fail** operation; and for write access during the **trail** operation. Unlike choice points, the size of the block of memory accessed during one of these operations is not fixed. Write accesses tend to trickle in one word at a time; while read accesses occur in bursts. The size of the burst is dynamically determined by how many items were trailed since the current choice point state was last restored. This behavior makes it difficult to fix a size for a trail buffer. In addition, due to the nature of the trail, once a read access to a trail entry is made, it will never be attempted again. This precludes any opportunity for revalidating an invalid or empty trail buffer from memory without added effort. Simulation results show that only 6% of all memory reads are to the trail. Thus trail buffering seems an inefficient use of space and hardware resources.

Read and write references to the current environment are not localized to a few instances in the microcode, but occur throughout many of the macro instructions as references to **Y** registers. Many of these references are easily identifiable as current environment references, however; due to dereferencing, a random class reference may write to a current environment location, creating consistency problems between a buffer and memory. Invalidation of a current environment buffer is localized to a single instance, namely the **deallocate** instruction. However, the entire environment is never accessed as a block, as in the case of choice points in a **fail** operation. This again would preclude revalidating the environment buffer without added effort. In addition, environments are variable in size (though an upper bound of 256 **Y** registers is imposed by the instruction format). Environments may even vary in size dynamically due to the trimming feature of the PLM. Therefore, management of an environment buffer would be considerably more complex than the choice point cache. Simulation results show that 12% of all memory reads are statically identifiable as reads to the current environment. Environment buffering is deemed not feasible for the current design.

The effect of a trail and environment buffer can be realized with a general data cache mechanism. Due to space considerations on this design, such a scheme was not investigated.

CHAPTER SUMMARY

This Chapter has described the microarchitecture of the PLM. The three major components of the microarchitecture, the Prefetch Unit, Data path and Microengine, were discussed in detail. For each of these components consideration was given to the physical hardware to realize the features described. The form of the microcode was also discussed as well as the tuning of the microcode to the data path and the tuning of the data path to the microcode. Finally a discussion of the considerations for memory access in the PLM was provided.

CHAPTER 5

THE EXPERIMENT

The PLM is an experiment in the design of a specialized processor for Prolog and its implementation in hardware. This Chapter describes the tests used to evaluate the effectiveness of the design features and hardware of the PLM described in Chapter 4. The methodology of the experiment is first described. Results of the experiment presented in this Chapter were generated from the simulators for the PLM. Two levels of simulation were performed: Level 1 at the ISA Level and Level 2 at the Register Transfer Level. The simulators are described together with the simplifying assumptions made in their implementation. The set of Benchmark programs used to evaluate the PLM is briefly described here. An analysis of the results of the experiments is provided including the effects of cdr-coding, environment trimming, sidetracking, and host memory and processing speeds. A case study of variations on compiling code for the PLM is provided as well as an analysis and critique of the PLM data path and microcode.

METHODOLOGY

The development of the PLM was an experimental process which took place over a period of three years. This process, undertaken in a top down manner, began with studies at the high level of abstraction represented by the work of Kowalski [35] on the definition of logic as a programming language and proceeded to the selection of Prolog as an instance of such a language. At the next, more detailed level of abstraction, the work of Warren [63, 64] on the definition of an abstract machine for Prolog provided an excellent starting point for conducting an experiment at evaluating the effectiveness of a specialized architecture for Prolog under the real world constraints imposed by physical hardware.

The experimental method used in this research consisted of the development of a set of tools, each at a more detailed level of abstraction, and the use of those tools for testing the hypotheses on the principles and features required to implement a high performance architecture for Prolog. Three such tools were developed; two software simulators and a hardware implementation of the PLM. The first simulator, Level 1, is an ISA simulator of the instruction set which was used to understand and evaluate the operations required to implement Prolog. The second simulator, Level 2, is a Register Transfer simulator of the microarchitecture of the PLM which was used to develop and evaluate the implementation strategies of the ISA. The simulators are described in the next section. The final and most detailed tool developed was the hardware of the PLM. This step is most important as it verifies and validates the concepts developed in the simulators by showing that they can be realized in a real, physical machine.

A hardware implementation of the PLM as described in Chapter 4 was built and tested. The machine consisted of three VAX hex cards, two for the processor and one for the PMI, consisting of approximately 600 TTL MSI and LSI parts. The system was interfaced to an NCR 9300 system with 4 MBytes of memory which acted as the host. The processor was tested with a 10 MHz clock and verified for a few small test programs. However, the memory interface to the NCR was not completely functional and the lack of software support for the NCR precluded full testing of the hardware system.

The processor architecture and microcode were verified using the Xenologic Incorporated Model X-1 system [18] interfaced to a SUN 3/160 workstation acting as the host. The design of the X-1 is a variation on the PLM described here, being significantly different in the memory interface. Nevertheless, the X-1 provided a second verification of the feasibility of many of the ideas presented in the previous Chapters for implementation in a real machine, particularly some that were developed after the PLM hardware was constructed.

THE SIMULATORS

The PLM architecture has been simulated at two levels of detail. The Level 1 simulator models at the ISA level and the Level 2 simulator models at the microarchitecture level. In addition to providing execution of PLM assembly code, the simulators provide a debugging facility for monitoring and debugging the execution of compiled Prolog programs and an instrumentation package for measuring the performance and behavior patterns of the design. The simulators are written in the C language [33] and run on a VAX11/750 under Berkeley (4.2 BSD) Unix[†]. Details of the features available from the simulators can be found in Dobry [20].

ISA Simulation - Level 1.

The Level 1 simulator models the PLM at the ISA level with each PLM macroinstruction implemented by a C routine. This simulator was useful in verifying the correctness of the semantics of individual instructions and in debugging compiled code.

The simulator provides the facilities for loading and executing compiled programs in assembly language, as well as debugging facilities to observe registers and memory as execution proceeds. All of the programmer visible processor registers are represented together with arrays representing the various memory

---

[†] Unix is a Trademark of Bell Laboratories.

areas in the architecture.

The simulator begins by initializing several internal tables from files which specify the instruction set and the built-in predicates known to the system. Next the Code Space is loaded from an assembly language file containing the code of the program being executed. During this load, two additional tables are constructed; one mapping procedure names to Code Space addresses and the other mapping labels. The Code Space is represented as an array of structures, each element containing one PLM instruction. The instructions are stored as strings in two parts; the opcode string and the argument list string.

The basic loop of the simulator consists of calls to a dispatch routine either directly or from the debugger. The dispatch routine examines the opcode string of the instruction pointed to by the modeled P register and invokes the appropriate instruction subroutine. Each of these C subroutines models the entire microroutine of an instruction and consist of two parts; the *top* and the *bottom*. The *top* completes the decode of the instruction by examining the argument list string and extracting operands or operand specifiers. The *bottom* performs the actual ISA level register transfers and memory operations dictated by the instruction.

The Level 1 simulator also provides debugging facilities to allow single stepping, setting of breakpoints, and control flow guidance from the user. In addition, processor registers and memory areas may be examined. Finally the simulator provides an instrumentation package to measure the behavior of executing programs.

RTL Simulation - Level 2.

The Level 2 simulator models the PLM at the microarchitecture level with each microinstruction implemented as a C routine. This level of simulation is useful for measuring the performance of the design and for observing how changes to the design affect the performance. The simulator provides a more detailed model of the

PLM architecture. Here all processor registers in the data path are represented. The kernel of the Level 2 simulator is essentially the same as the Level 1. The major differences being with the C subroutines modeling the instructions. The *top* of these routines remain unchanged from the Level 1. They are invoked by the dispatch routine at each instruction boundary, i.e. at the start of processing of a new macroinstruction. The *bottom* of these subroutines simply branch to the entry point microstate routine for the instruction. The operations performed by the bottom of a Level 1 routine are now performed by a sequence of C subroutines each representing a microstate of the processor. Each microstate routine models the register transfers that take place in one cycle over the data paths of the PLM. In the Level 2 simulator each loop through the dispatch routine corresponds to one cycle of the PLM with the next state being determined by the microengine model.

From the above discussion, it can be seen that the collection of microstate routines of the Level 2 simulator is the microcode of the PLM written in C. A set of Unix utilities is used to translate these C routines into flowcharts representing the microcode. A further collection of Unix utility calls then translates these flowcharts into the microcode bits loaded into the proms making up the microstore of the PLM hardware.

The debugger of the Level 2 simulator provides the same facilities as that of the Level 1 with the added capability of setting a microbreakpoint. The instrumentation package of the Level 2 simulator provides those features of Level 1 as well as such timing information as total clock ticks, Prolog engine bus utilization, and prefetch behavior.

The baseline model in the level 2 simulator makes several simplifying assumptions. For example, memory accesses are assumed to take a single clock cycle and instruction prefetch is assumed to be perfect (i.e. no wait is ever required for instruction fetch). Built-in functions implemented via the escape mechanism are not accurately timed; a standard three cycles is allotted for these operations (the benchmark set uses only very simple built-in functions so this assumption is not unreasonable). The operations performed by the PMI are not simulated directly by the Level 2 simulator but their effects may be measured via switches which activate models of these operations to act on the clock counter of the simulator. For example, the Prefetch Unit may be modeled to include processor stalls due to jump instructions. A more realistic memory access time of three cycles, corresponding to the access time of the NCR/32, may also be selected as well as separate switches to enable models for the Write Buffer (and associated processor stalls for data reads) and the Choice Point Cache to measure the effect on performance of the system. Measurements with the level 2 simulator with its simplest set of assumptions are referred to as baseline performance.

THE BENCHMARK SET

An analysis of the effects of architectural features on performance of the PLM must be accomplished by means of benchmarking [52]. Any set of benchmark programs cannot cover a myriad of Prolog applications, however a representative set of typical operations common in Prolog programs can give a rough picture of the expected performance of the machine. In addition, to verify the correctness of the microcode, benchmarks must be selected which exercise the microcode completely. The benchmarks used in the experiments were selected to attempt to meet both of these goals with primary emphasis on the later. Results presented in the next section were obtained from the level 2 simulator and are best interpreted in comparing the performance of the PLM against itself with and without various architectural features and compilation techniques.

Before describing the results of the benchmark programs, a brief discussion of what is measured is warranted. In general, a benchmark program consists of some initial setup code to initialize the problem followed by a call of the predicate performing the test operation. This initialization code corresponds to the top level query posed to the Prolog program. To verify correct performance, upon return from the test operation the results are written to the screen. The execution times presented here are measured from the call to the test predicate to its return. Initialization and result output are not measured. Times are expressed in cycles and milliseconds assuming a 10MHz processor and performance is expressed in KLIPS (Kilo Logical Inferences per Second). An inference is counted as an invocation of a Prolog subgoal. This corresponds to the number of **call**, **execute**, and **escape** instructions executed during the timed interval. Caution should be used in interpreting the performance numbers as the amount of "work" done for an individual inference is highly variable and problem dependent.

RESULTS

This section describes the results of benchmark testing for the PLM. Results were generated by the level 2 simulator, and in general, under the simpifying assumptions discussed above. For studies of the effects of various features of the PLM, measurements are made with respect to the baseline performance results.

Determinate concat - A Case Study.

The list concatenation benchmark has become a frequently quoted Prolog system comparison benchmark as performance numbers are available for a large number of systems. The benchmark is the concatenation of two lists to form a third; however, the length of the lists being joined is not generally specified. The Prolog code for the concat predicate is

```
concat([],L,L).
concat([X|L1],L2,[X|L3]) :- concat(L1,L2,L3).
```

In the determinate case, the second clause of concat recursively
"cdr's" down the list in the first argument copying it to the top of
the Heap and binding the resulting list to the unbound variable in
the third argument. When the end of the first list is encountered,
the first clause binds the tail of the list being built to the list in the
second argument. The standard compilation for concat is shown in
Figure 5.1. A study of the behavior of this code shows that for the
PLM, performance, in KLIPS, can be predicted by:

$$P(inKLIPS) = K \frac{n+1}{bn+c}$$

where

n is the number of elements in the list in the first argument

b is the number of cycles executed for the second clause

c is the number of cycles executed for the first clause

and K is the conversion factor for KLIPS, 10^4 for a 10 MHz
processor.

In the limit, for large lists, the performance for determinate concat
is:

$$\frac{1}{b}$$

The level 2 simulator shows 39 cycles for **b** giving a limit for performance of 256 KLIPS under the baseline memory and prefetch
assumptions. More realistically, the **switch_on_term** instruction
causes a stall of the processor while the Prefetch Unit fetches and
partially decodes the target instruction. Assuming a stall of 5
cycles gives b becomes 44 cycles and a performance limit of 227
KLIPS.

To improve these performance limits, the objective is to
make **b** smaller, even at the expense of **c**. One approach, given
that concat will always be invoked determinately (i.e. with bound
first and second arguments and unbound third), is to compile concat without the stalling **switch_on_term** instruction using the

```
procedure concat
        switch_on_term C1,C2,fail

C1a:    try_me_else   C2a          % concat(
C1:     get_nil       A1           % [],
        get_value     A2,A3        % L,L
        proceed                    % ).

C2a:    trust_me_else fail         % concat(
C2:     get_list      A1           % [
        unify_variable X4          % X
        unify_cdr     A1           % |L1],L2,
        get_list      A3           % [
        unify_value   X4           % X
        unify_cdr     A3           % |L3])
        execute         concat % :- concat(L1,L2,L3).
```

Figure 5.1: Compiled code for concat.

sidetracking technique described earlier. Figure 5.2 shows the compiled code for concat with sidetracking.

With the sidetracking operation in place, **b** becomes 33 cycles and the limit on performance is 303 KLIPS.

A second approach is to compile concat using a **put_list** instruction to do the copying to the top of the Heap. From the declarative semantics of Prolog, the code for concat is seen to copy the list in the first argument one element at a time to the top of the Heap. On each recursive call, and unbound cdr is left at the end of the list copied so far to be bound on the next iteration. As long as

---

```
procedure concat
        try_me_else    C3|tvar            % create short choice point

CC:     get_list       A1                 % concat( [
        unify_variable X4                 %        X
        unify_cdr      A1                 %              |L1],L2,
        get_list       A3                 %     [
        unify_value    X4                 %     X
        unify_cdr      A3                 %       |L3])
        execute              ccon         % :- concat(L1,L2,L3).

C3:     trust_me_else  fail               % remove short choice point
        get_nil        A1                 % concat( [],
        get_value      A2,A3              % L,L
        proceed                           % ).
```

Figure 5.2: Compiling concat with sidetracking

---

no other data is placed on the Heap between recursions, this unbound cdr is not necessary. Figure 5.3 shows a version of compiled code which uses **put_list** to copy an element and avoid the unbound cdr and the overhead of binding and trail checking on the next iteration. In this code somewhat radical changes have been made, however it uses only existing instructions, albeit in nonstandard ways. A brief description of this code is in order. The **get_list** instruction at the entry to concat is to be executed only on the initial call to bind the variable in the third argument to a list. The entry point for recursive calls then moves to the label CC. The **switch_on_term** fails for a variable in argument 1 as this is not allowed in the determinate case. A jump to an error handler

---

```
procedure concat
        get_list          X3              % bind output arg to a list
CC:     switch_on_term    C1,C2,fail      % test first arg
        fail                              % non-determinate case, fail

C2:     get_list          X1              % unify with first list
        unify_variable X4                 % X is in X4
        unify_cdr         X1
        put-list          X3              % write X to top of Heap
        unify_value       X4
        execute           CC              % recur to alt entry point

C1:     get_nil           X1              % termination condition
        unify_cdr         X3              % put unbnd cdr on result list
        get_value         X2,X3           % bind second arg to rslt cdr
        proceed
```

Figure 5.3: Explicit copying concat

---

may also be used here, but the code shown does not completely test the entry mode dynamically. The code for the second clause begins as before (at C2) processing the list in the first argument in read mode. The code to process the third argument uses **put_list** to force the PLM into write mode so that the **unify_value** will write the next element at the top of the Heap. The **execute** instruction then recurs to the alternate entry point. When the end of the first list is encountered, the code for the first clause begins with the **get_nil** as before, however, now an unbound cdr is needed at the end of the copied list to be bound to the list in argument 2. The **unify_cdr** instruction creates this variable (the PLM is still in write mode from the last iteration) and the **get_value** does the binding.

The code in Figure 5.3 relies on a very detailed understanding of the effects of each instruction and of the operation being performed by concat. As such the technique may be beyond the capability of current compiler technology. However, such a precompiled predicate can be provided in a library available to a programmer for superior performance, in this case, a limit of 400 KLIPS (333 KLIPS with the stall). Sidetracking may also be applied to this code for further improvement (526 KLIPS).

One final improvement to concat needs mention. The list copy operation can be implemented in microcode as an internal built-in and concat compiled as shown in Figure 5.4. For this code the *l_copy* built-in is used to copy the list in X1 to the top of the Heap leaving an unbound variable at the end. The built-in leaves a pointer to the copied list in X1 and a variable pointer to the unbound cdr in X2. The two **get_value** instructions unify the results for concat. For the list copy operation in microcode, **b** is 4 cycles. However, in this case the concept of inferences is blurred somewhat. With the strict definition provided earlier, only one inference is counted regardless of the size of the list. However, the effective number of inferences may be set by the Prolog code for concat. Therefore, with the list copy operation, the limit on performance is 2.5 Effective MLIPS. (With a minor microcode change, **b** can be reduced to 3 cycles giving 3.3 Effective MLIPS; and with a microarchitecture change a list element can be copied in 2 cycles for 5 Effective MLIPS).

An added advantage in the last two examples is that they generate cdr-compressed versions of the copied list. This will speed up processing of the resultant lists as will be seen in the next section.

The performance projected in these examples is a best-case analysis. Perfect memory and prefetch behavior were assumed and the limit on performance for very large lists was derived.

```
procedure concat
        switch_on_term C1,C2,fail    % test first arg
        fail                         % non-determinate case, fail

C2:     get_variable   X4,X2         % move second arg to X4
        escape         l_copy        % copy 1st list to top of Heap
        get_value      X4,X2         % bind 2nd arg to cdr of rslt
        get_value      X3,X1         % bind 3rd arg to result
        proceed

C1:     get_nil        X1            % covers empty list case
        get_value      X2,X3
        proceed
```

Figure 5.4: List Copy concat

This section has shown several examples of variations on compiling concat for improved performance (a factor of 2 with existing instructions; an order of magnitude with specialized microcode). This is summarized in Table 5.1. These techniques and others are not restricted to concat, but may be applied to other predicates given sufficient additional information such as modes. These examples illustrate the robustness of the instruction set and microarchitecture and show there is room for vast improvement in compiler technology. The Table also shows the types of "games" that can be played with benchmark programs. A lesson to be learned from this case study is that quoting a single performance number for a benchmark is not necessarily indicative of the real performance of the machine.

Technique	Performance (KLIPS)	
	no stall	stall
Standard	256	227
Sidetracking	303	303
Explicit list copy	400	333
Explicit list copy + Sidetracking	526	526
Microcode list copy	2500	2500

Table 5.1: Summary of concat Performance

The Effects of cdr-coding.

This section discusses the benefits and shortcomings of cdr-coding lists in the PLM. When cdr-coding was introduced in Chapter 3, the emphasis was on space savings on the Heap. A cdr-compressed list requires half of the space used to represent a list that a structure-based representation uses. The space requirements of a fully cdr-expanded list is the same as the structure-based representation, namely two words per list element. Thus cdr-coding provides heap requirements that are no worse than non-cdr-coded schemes and may be considerably better in some cases.

A second advantage for cdr-coding lies in the instruction sequences for processing lists. For construction or unification of multi-element lists, the number of instructions executed with a cdr-coding scheme is approximately one third of the number for a structure-based scheme. The smaller number of instructions results in fewer cycles to construct or unify the list. Consider the clause head:

$$f([a, b, c]) :- ...$$

Table 5.2 shows the compiled code for head unification for both a cdr-coded scheme (Table 5.2a) and a structure-based scheme (Table 5.2b). Also shown are the number of cycles executed by the PLM in both read mode (the predicate invoked with a list) and write mode (the predicate invoked with an unbound variable). For the structure-based scheme in read mode, cycle counts are provided for the "unify" instructions as they exist (supporting cdr-coding) and as they would be with the removal of cdr-coding support. (It should be noted that both of these instructions sequences can be made to run on the PLM*, with the code in Table 5.2b simply not taking advantage of cdr-coding. As such, cdr-coding may be considered a compiler option as long as its use is consistent throughout the code). An otherwise identical microarchitecture is assumed. For the cdr-coded scheme in read mode, cycle counts are provided for both the case of a cdr-compressed list and a fully cdr-expanded list. These represent the best and worst cases for cdr-coding.

A few remarks are in order. The large number of cycles for **get_list** in write mode are due to the dereference operation on the unbound variable (passed in the first call and created by the "unify_variable X8" in subsequent calls) and the trail check operation when the variable is bound to a list. The variable passed in is assumed to be on the Stack so the trail check operation is shorter. Techniques for reducing the number of cycles for these operations are discussed at the end of the Chapter.

For multi-element list construction, for example in the clause segment

---

* To run on the PLM the "unify_nil" instruction would be replaced by "unify_constant nil" with no loss in performance.

Instruction	Cycles		
	Read		Write
	compressed	expanded	
get_list X1	3	3	12
unify_constant a	3	3	3
unify_constant b	3	3	3
unify_constant c	3	3	3
unify_nil	3	3	3
Total	15	15	24

a. Cdr-coded Execution (cycles)

Instruction	Cycles		
	Read		Write
	as is	corrected	
get_list X1	3	3	12
unify_constant a	3	3	3
unify_variable X8	5	4	4
get_list X8	3	3	13
unify_constant b	3	3	3
unify_variable X8	5	4	4
get_list X8	3	3	13
unify_constant c	3	3	3
unify_nil	3	3	3
Total	31	29	58

b. Structure-based Execution (cycles)

Table 5.2: Multi-element List Unification

$$\dots \ :\text{-} \dots , f(\ [\ a, \ b, \ c \ ] \ ), \ \dots$$

the code is similar with the first **get_list** instruction replaced with a **put_list** (3 cycles). For the structure-based scheme the other **get_list** instructions remain.

The data in Table 5.2 shows that for processing a list more than one element at a time, cdr-coding has a decided advantage in time. This type of processing also produces cdr-compressed lists realizing a space advantage as well. However, in Prolog programs, lists are often processed one element at a time and recursively. For example, in the benchmark set used here, of 182 clauses only 57 do some form of list processing and only 19 process lists more than one element at a time. A typical example of recursive, single-element list processing is found in concat. Table 5.3 shows an execution trace for the standard compilation of one iteration of the concat loop in the determinate case. The instruction cycle counts are provided as above except that mode is determined dynamically. Again cdr-coded and structure-based cases are considered. The particular iteration shown is other than the first call to concat so that the **get_list** in write mode is to a variable on the Heap. (Note: no Prefetch Unit stall for **switch_on_term** is included but it would be the same in both cases. Also **execute** takes zero cycles as it is executed by the Prefetch Unit).

The data shows that the cdr-coding code is slightly better than the structure-based code with the existing microcode but realizes a one cycle loss per loop with respect to an implementation with no cdr-coding support. Another surprising result is that the cdr-compressed and cdr-expanded cases require the same number of cycles. A close study with the level 2 simulator reveals what is happening.

The extra cycle in the cdr-coded case is in the **unify_variable** instruction in read mode. The five cycles in this instruction perform the following operations:

Instruction		Cycles	
		compressed	expanded
switch_on_term		6	6
get_list X1	(read)	3	3
unify_variable X4	(read)	5	5
unify_cdr X1	(read)	4	4
get_list X3	(write)	13	13
unify_value X4	(write)	4	4
unify_cdr X3	(write)	4	4
execute concat		0	0
Total		39	39

a. Cdr-coded Execution (cycles)

Instruction		Cycles	
		as is	corrected
switch_on_term		6	6
get_list X1	(read)	3	3
unify_variable X4	(read)	5	4
unify_variable X1	(read)	5	4
get_list X3	(write)	13	13
unify_value X4	(write)	4	4
unify_variable X3	(write)	4	4
execute concat		0	0
Total		40	38

b. Structure-based Execution (cycles)

Table 5.3: Single Element List Processing

(1)   Load the Memory Address Register (MAR) with the address of the next element.

(2)   Read memory.

(3)   Branch on the cdr-bit of the returned data.

(4)   Put the data away in the Xi register.

(5)   Prefetch the next instruction and do an IFETCH call. (This cycle can be eliminated as will be shown in a later section but would be eliminated for the structure-based case as well).

In the case of concat, and most others, a cdr-tagged item will not be read from memory (the cdr would have been read by the previous iteration **unify_cdr**). A cdr-tagged item would only appear for cases with cdr chains of length greater than one which only occurs in unusual, complex list construction code. Therefore, a common microprogramming technique may be applied here: bias the instruction to the most frequent case. Here cycles 3) and 4) may be done at the same time. If a cdr-tagged item is read, the Xi register will have the wrong value but can be corrected before completion of the instruction. With this change to the microcode, the **unify_variable** in read mode will be the same as the structure-based case.

For the cdr-compressed case, the simulator shows the following. On one iteration through the loop, the **unify_cdr** instruction in read mode must read the next list element to see if it is a cdr-tagged item. If it is cdr-tagged, the data is placed in the Xi register and the S register is updated. In the compressed case, the data is not cdr-tagged (the next car immediately follows the current one) so a list tagged pointer is constructed from the S register and placed in the Xi register. On the next iteration, the **unify_variable** instruction processing the car element reads the element a second time. Thus a compressed list saves neither time nor memory accesses. A minor modification to the microarchitecture allows the **unify_cdr** instruction to save the car element it read in a processor scratch register and flag the next iteration that the data is already available. Thus the next **unify_variable** instruction can perform the following operations:

(1)   Load the MAR and test if data is already present.

(2)   If data is available (compressed case) put it away in the Xi register.

(3)   Prefetch the next instruction and do an IFETCH call.

With these changes, Table 5.3a is modified as shown in Table 5.4. Thus for one-element-at-a-time processing with cdr-coding, no time is lost in the worst case and a single cycle per element may be saved for compressed lists. With only a single scratch register available the data forwarding technique described above can be used only once per loop so that if multiple lists are being processed in read mode in a single clause, others will require an additional cycle to read the car a second time but this is still no worse than the structure-based case.

As was noted earlier, concat itself, and other predicates which construct lists recursively one element at a time, generate partially expanded lists. Several techniques were provided in the last section for generating compressed lists, but in general lists may tend toward the cdr-expanded state. However, as was the case for space, the cdr-coding scheme provides no worse performance in time than the structure-based scheme and may provided improvement in some cases.

In the final analysis on cdr-coding, for multi-element list processing, cdr-coding provides a significant savings in both time and space. For the more frequent one-element-at-a-time processing, cdr-coding is no worse and may show slight gains over a non-cdr-coded implementation; all this at the expense of a little hardware in the microarchitecture and a little care in writing the microcode.

Instruction		Cycles	
		compressed	expanded
switch_on_term		6	6
get_list X1	(read)	3	3
unify_variable X4	(read)	3	4
unify_cdr X1	(read)	4	4
get_list X3	(write)	13	13
unify_value X4	(write)	4	4
unify_cdr X3	(write)	4	4
execute concat		0	0
Total		37	38

Table 5.4: Corrected Cdr-coding Microcode

The Effects of Environment Trimming.

The ability of the WAM to trim the size of an environment dynamically as processing progresses through the subgoals was originally described by Warren [64] and was discussed in Chapter 2. The implementation of this feature in the PLM was discussed in Chapter 3. The primary function of environment trimming is to reduce the size of the Stack. However, as is the case for deallocating environments, when an environment is trimmed, the size of the stack may not be immediately reduced. If the trimmed environment is before the current choice point on the stack, the Y register locations trimmed would be "deallocated" but not reclaimed. This section describes an experiment which was run to test the effectiveness of environment trimming.

Four benchmark programs were selected which used environment trimming. They are *quicksort*, *query*, *queens*, and *browse*.

The compiled code for these benchmarks was hand modified to negate environment trimming by modifying the N operands of **call** instructions and by replacing the **put_unsafe_value** instructions used to processed the trimmed Y register with **put_value** instructions. The resulting code was run on the Level 2 simulator. The maximum Stack size and execution speed in KLIPS with and without environment trimming is shown in Table 5.5. As can be seen, only one benchmark, *quicksort*, realized any stack size savings at all. The savings is due to the first clause of the *qsort* procedure:

qsort([X|L],R,R0) :-
          partition(L,X,L1,L2),
          qsort(L2,R1,R0),
          qsort(L1,R,[X|R1]).

Benchmark	Stack Size (words)		Speed (KLIPS)	
	with	without	with	without
quicksort	75	85	137.3	138.2
query	57	57	166.6	168.7
queens	412	412	138.4	139.2
browse	749	749	100.3	100.6

Table 5.5: The Effects of Environment Trimming

In this clause the environment may be trimmed by two variables (L1 and R0) before the first recursive call to *qsort*. Because *partition* terminates determinately (i.e. leaves no choice point on the Stack when it returns) the environment for *qsort* is at the top of the Stack when the variables are trimmed and as a result the size of the Stack is reduced.

However, Table 5.5 also shows that in all cases a slight performance advantage is gained when environment trimming is eliminated. This is due to the difference between **put_value** and **put_unsafe_value**. Recall that

put_value   Yi,Xj

simply reads Yi and places the value in Xj. On the other hand, **put_unsafe_value** must read Yi, and if it is a variable, dereference it and check to see if it is an unbound variable in the current environment, indicating an unsafe variable. An unsafe variable must then be moved to the heap. Even if the variable is safe, the added check makes **put_unsafe_value** take longer than **put_value**. It should be noted that a smart compiler with mode information may be able to determine when **put_unsafe_value** may be relaced by **put_value** at compile time even with environment trimming. For example, this is the case with *qsort* as R0 resides outside the current environment (it occurs in the head) and L1 will be bound by partition. However this may not always be the case, particularly when incomplete mode information is available.

From this data, the effectiveness of environment trimming is questionable. Real Stack space savings are small and may be realized in only very restricted cases. In addition, the expense of using **put_unsafe_value** may invoke a performance penalty. In this light, future implementations of the PLM should not include environment trimming.

The Effects of Sidetracking.

The sidetracking technique was described in Chapter 3. The compiled code of six of the benchmark programs to which sidetracking could be applied was hand modified and run on the simulator. The benchmarks were *concat, naive reverse, serialize, quicksort, queens,* and *browse.* This section summarizes the results of these tests.

Table 5.6 shows the overall performance results for these benchmarks. Shown are the number of inferences counted and the performance in KLIPS for the standard compiled form of the benchmarks, i.e. with no sidetracking. For sidetracking, two sets of data are presented. The Normal CP column shows the performance and percent speed-up realized when only a short failure operation is performed with full choice points created. The Short

Benchmark		Std	Sidetracking			
			Normal CP		Short CP	
Name	Inf	KLIPS	KLIPS	%	KLIPS	%
concat	31	239.1	269.1	12.4	271.5	13.4
n-reverse	497	231.7	249.1	7.5	252.9	9.2
Average				10.0		11.3
quicksort	609	137.3	157.9	15.0	167.8	22.2
serialize	322	131.2	148.2	13.0	154.3	17.6
queens	243905	138.4	167.3	20.9	176.3	27.4
browse	44872	100.4	131.7	31.2	138.8	38.3
Average				20.0		26.3
Overall				16.7		21.4

Table 5.6: The Effects of sidetracking

CP column shows the performance and percent speed-up when short choice points are created for sidetracking as well. This is full sidetracking. The improvement for full sidetracking is obviously due to the elimination of memory writes to the choice points. The data shown here is for single cycle memory access.

The speed-ups over standard compilation shown in Table 5.6 can be seen to be due to two effects. For the determinate benchmarks such as *concat* and *naive reverse* speed-up is due to the reduction of the instructions executed in the loop of the recursive calls, in particular the elimination of the explicit loop termination test. In these cases an average 11.3% speed-up is realized. This effect is seen to be smaller than the effect for non-determinate, search-type, benchmarks. In these cases, the effect is due to the reduction in the time spent processing choice points that exist in both the standard and sidetracking code as well as the elimination of redundant head unification in sidetracking code. These savings represent a 26.3% speed-up for sidetracking.

Data supporting the discussion above is shown in Table 5.7. Here the percent improvements in memory reads and writes, choice point reads and writes, and instructions executed for full sidetracking over standard compilation is presented.

For determinate benchmarks, a net increase in the number of memory operations is seen by the negative savings figures. This increase is due to the processing of choice points in the sidetracking code where none was present in the standard code. However, the savings in instructions executed offsets the extra memory references to produce a net speed-up in performance.

For the non-determinate benchmarks, the savings in instructions executed is only slightly better than the determinate case. However, the savings in memory operations, particularly choice point reads and writes, is dramatic - approximately two thirds of choice point accesses and approximately 45% of all memory accesses are eliminated by sidetracking. (It should be noted that

Benchmark	% Change for Sidetracking vs Standard				
	Memory Access		CP Access		Instrs
	Read	Write	Read	Write	Exec
concat	-3.2	-2.0	-	-	9.3
n-reverse	-4.9	-4.6	-	-	8.4
Average	-4.1	-3.3			8.9
quicksort	38.2	49.6	67.7	80.0	14.3
serialize	33.7	36.5	71.2	62.5	12.6
queens	58.6	59.8	75.9	79.3	12.6
browse	42.9	41.9	56.6	56.4	23.3
Average	43.4	47.0	67.9	69.5	15.7
Overall	27.6	30.2			13.4

Table 5.7: Sidetracking Memory and Instruction Data(%)

not all of the memory operation savings are due to choice points. Savings are also realized by the elimination of memory accesses for redundant head unification steps).

From the data it can be seen that significant speed-ups can be realized by applying the sidetracking technique (an overall average of 21.4%). For determinate programs the effect is smaller (11.3% vs 26.3%) and may be eroded by disparities between processor cycle time and memory access time. As the number of processor cycles required for a memory operation increases, the added memory operations for choice points in sidetracking code may cause a relative slow-down with respect to standard code. However, for non-determinate programs, the dramatic savings in memory operations enhances the relative speed-ups for large disparities between processor and memory speeds.

The Effects of Host and Memory Speed.

The PLM is designed as an attached coprocessor relying on some host for memory support and for processing built-in predicates beyond the capabilities of its own functional unit. This section describes the effects on the performance of the PLM as the memory access time and host processor speed are varied. The data in this section assumes no buffers or caches are present between the PLM and memory. The next section analyzes the effects of buffers and caches on performance for a fixed memory access time.

The PLM is a memory intensive processor. Over the benchmark programs, on average, a memory access is requested every 3.6 cycles. Because of the state saving operations involved in non-deterministic processing, memory reads and writes occur with approximately equal frequency. The memory access behavior is summarized in Table 5.8.

Table 5.9 shows the performance, in KLIPS, for the ten benchmark programs. Memory access times of 1, 3, 10, 30, and 50 PLM cycles are presented. Figure 5.5 shows a plot of average performance as a function of memory access time. The data indicates a substantial penalty in performance for slower memory access, even at the low end of the scale. The Write Buffer and Choice Point Cache of the PMI provide a method for realizing an effective access time close to one PLM cycle. Their effects are analyzed in the next section.

The processing of built-in predicates has been shown to have a significant effect on overall performance in two studies done at ECRC [49] and ICOT [46]. The ECRC study performed a static analysis of 32 benchmark programs (including some of the benchmarks presented here) of varying size from small to large. The ICOT study performed a static analysis of 33 benchmarks as well as a dynamic analysis of two large programs. Both studies showed similar static results of 45% to 50% of goals being evaluable

Bmk	Cycles	Reads	Writes	Cyc/ Acc	Cyc/ Read	Cyc/ Write
concat	1295	121	92	6.1	10.7	14.1
n-reverse	21453	2041	1666	5.8	10.5	12.9
quicksort	44360	6176	8610	3.0	7.2	5.2
serialize	24536	3905	2856	3.6	6.3	8.6
differen	7702	685	1758	3.2	11.2	4.4
query	171349	26001	26292	3.3	6.6	6.5
queens	17619586	3946938	2453253	2.8	4.5	7.2
mumath	93404	17195	14581	2.9	5.4	6.4
circuit	72169	17143	9794	2.7	4.2	7.4
browse	4399420	836089	683482	2.9	5.3	6.4
Average				3.6	7.2	7.9

Table 5.8: Memory Reference Behavior

Benchmark	Performance (KLIPS)				
	Memory Access Time (cycles)				
	1	3	10	30	50
concat	239.4	180.1	96.5	41.5	26.4
naive reverse	231.7	172.2	90.7	38.5	24.5
quicksort	137.3	82.4	34.3	12.9	7.9
serialize	131.2	84.6	37.7	14.6	9.1
differen	85.7	52.4	22.2	8.4	5.2
query	166.6	103.4	44.5	16.9	10.4
queens	138.4	80.2	32.4	12.0	7.4
mumath	136.5	81.2	33.6	12.6	7.7
circuit	97.1	55.6	22.3	8.2	5.0
browse	102.0	50.1	22.9	9.0	5.6
Average	146.6	94.2	43.7	17.5	10.9

Table 5.9: The Effects of Memory Access Time

predicates. (Evaluable predicates are a superset of the built-ins discussed here. They include predicates handled by PLM instructions, such as **cut**, or a sequence of PLM instructions such as for *var*. The data presented here is for predicates for which an **escape** instruction is generated for the PLM). Among the most frequent evaluable predicates in both studies are I/O and arithmetic predicates. However in the dynamic analysis, the ICOT study shows the convenience and arithmetic predicates as the most frequently executed with the I/O among the least frequent. An important conclusion to be drawn is that the speed of execution of evaluable predicates can strongly effect the performance of a Prolog system.

From the above discussion, a study of escapes in the PLM is in order. In the baseline simulator, three cycles are used to model the execution time for a built-in invoked with an **escape**

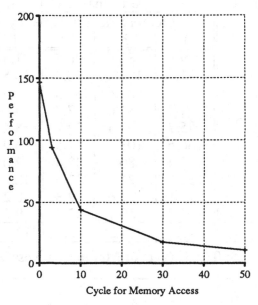

Figure 5.5: Performance vs Memory Access Time

instruction (in addition to the overhead of escape decoding). While this may be reasonable for many internal built-ins, an external built-in would require more time. The time for an external built-in is dependent on both the host CPU speed for executing the built-in operation and the interrupt processing time. The baseline data for the benchmark programs from the simulator was used to analyze the effect of host speed on PLM performance.

First a brief analysis of the benchmark programs is presented. In the baseline compiled code, **escape** instructions are 1.1% of the static instructions generated. This represents 34% of subgoal invocations. The built-ins used in the programs are shown below with the static fraction (%) of total escapes.

is	35
nl	30
write	21
<	6
>	3
integer	2
atom	2
length	2

Dynamically, the **escape** instruction represents 2.7% of instructions executed. For the performance data the I/O built-ins (write and nl) are not included as they occur outside the measured time for the benchmarks. Of the remaining built-ins, most of them could be implemented as internal built-ins, however for the data presented below, all escapes executed within the timed interval are assumed to be external.

Table 5.10 shows the performance (in KLIPS) for the benchmark programs with host response times of 3, 10, 100, 1000, and 10000 PLM cycles. The average performance is plotted on a semi-log scale in Figure 5.6. Data is presented only for the seven benchmarks which used escapes. The data shows only minor effects on performance for small numbers of cycles (i.e. for internal built-ins) and dramatic effects for large numbers of cycles as would be expected for external built-ins (on the order of 1000 PLM cycles is not unreasonable for host processing including interrupt processing). The data presented above provides strong motivation for implementing as many built-ins internally as possible.

Bmk	No. of	Performance (KLIPS)				
		Host Processing Time (cycles)				
	Escapes	3	10	100	1000	10000
quicksort	228	137.3	131.9	91.3	22.4	2.6
serialize	95	131.2	127.3	95.1	27.0	3.3
query	2151	166.6	151.4	74.7	12.3	1.3
queens	139552	138.4	130.2	77.9	15.6	1.7
mumath	10	136.5	136.4	135.1	123.3	65.9
circuit	41	97.1	96.7	92.0	62.0	14.5
browse	5153	100.4	99.6	90.3	46.7	8.0
Average		129.6	124.8	93.8	44.2	13.9

Table 5.10: The Effect of Host Speed

The Effects of Buffers and Caches.

The previous section discussed the effects of memory access time on PLM performance assuming no buffers and caches. This section describes the effects of the Write Buffer and Choice Point Cache incorporated in the PLM design assuming a more realistic, non-ideal memory access time. In addition, the effect of the Prefetch Unit is discussed.

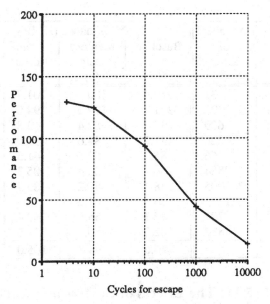

Figure 5.6: Performance vs Host Speed

Table 5.11 summarizes the results for buffers and caches. Column 1 shows the baseline performance of the PLM. Column 2 adds the realistic three cycle memory access time provided by the NCR system. The result is an average 36% slowdown with a high

Bmk	Number of Infer.	Performance (KLIPS)			
		Baseline (1)	Memory Data (2)	Write Buffer (3)	CP Cache (4)
concat	31	239.4	180.1	201.7	201.7
n-reverse	497	231.7	172.2	194.0	194.0
quicksort	609	137.3	82.4	93.8	100.6
serialize	322	131.2	84.6	91.9	99.4
differen	66	85.7	52.4	61.5	63.2
query	2854	166.6	103.4	105.3	128.0
queens	243905	138.4	80.2	85.7	104.7
mumath	1275	136.5	81.2	91.1	103.1
circuit	701	97.1	55.6	60.4	70.6
browse	44872	102.0	50.1	64.6	71.6
Average		146.6	94.2	105.0	113.7

Table 5.11: The Effects of Buffers and Caches

of 51% and a low of 25% from the ideal baseline model. Column 3 of Table 5.11 shows the resulting performance data when the Write Buffer is incorporated in the model. Under this model, memory write accesses require one cycle, while memory read accesses require at least 3 cycles and longer if the Write Buffer is not empty at the time of the read. The result is a 11% gain over column 2 (high 29%, low 2%) to 72% of base performance (high 84%, low 62%) Finally, Column 4 includes the Choice Point Cache to complete the modeling of the PLM design. The effectiveness of the Choice Point Cache can be shown to be due to the backtracking behavior of Prolog programs. Tick [57] has shown that shallow backtracking (backtracking to a choice point at the top of the Stack) is very frequent. The Choice Point Cache scheme presented here easily captures most shallow backtracking cases as well as many deep backtracking cases. The simulator results support this conclusion. It shows that for the benchmarks 46% of all memory reads are choice point reads, of which 87% are serviced by the cache. The misses in the Choice Point Cache are due to deep backtracking cases of failure in the last clause tried (following a "trust" instruction) or following a cut operation when the cache is invalid.

With the write buffer and Choice Point Cache an average of 113.7 KLIPS for these benchmarks represents a performance improvement of 21% over the realistic measurement of column 2 (high 43%, low 12%) and a realization of 78% of the baseline model (high 84%, low 70%).

The Prefetch Unit described in Chapter 4 was also modeled in the simulator. The model included the Instruction Buffer and an average case timing simulation for each of the instruction formats and types of fetch and alignment operations done by the Prefetch Unit. (The average was over the opcode positions in a 32 bit word read from memory). Memory access time for unaligned instructions and Prefetch Unit stalls for jump instructions were also modeled. For the data presented below, instruction memory access was assumed to occur without interference from data access.

Table 5.12 summarizes the results[*]. Again baseline performance is presented in column 1 (assuming perfect prefetch). Colunm 2 shows the performance for no Prefetch Unit installed. The data was generated by assuming one additional cycle is added to the execution time for each prefetch operation performed. This is a generous assumption; an estimate of average Prefetch Unit behavior shows 3 to 4 cycles to fetch and align an instruction. One cycle can be considered a realistic average for a non-compacted

---

[*] The data for the *browse* benchmark was not available for this analysis.

instruction storage in the Code Space. For the benchmarks, an average 21% slow down (high 33%, low 16%) is seen in column 2. In column 3 the results of the prefetch model are shown. On average for the benchmarks, realistic prefetch casues a 9% degradation from the baseline (high 15%, low 2%). The improvement in column 3 over column 2 reflects the Prefetch Unit's ability to fetch ahead of processor execution. Thus under the assumptions given, the Prefetch Unit represents a 12% speed-up for the PLM. Alternately, the 9% degradation of column 3 over column 1 reflects the processor stalls due to jump instructions. Finally, column 4 of Table 5.12 shows the projected performance of the PLM with the prefetch model, Write Buffer and Choice Point Cache present. The average 109.6 KLIPS represents 72% of the ideal performance (high 75%, low 68%). This represents the projected performance of the PLM under the conditions expected for the hardware.

A Critique of the PLM Microcode.

Besides the absolute performance numbers for the benchmark programs, the level 2 simulator provides other data which may be used to study the effectiveness of the microcode and microarchitecture for producing optimum performance. In this section a critical review of the PLM microcode, statically as well as dynamically, is discussed. Some problem areas are identified and possible solutions proposed.

As a first study, the microcode was examined statically to determine how well it utilized the various features of the microarchitecture including the busses, functional units, and microbranching capabilities. The results are summarized in Table 5.13. In the Table, columns are provided for each of the six classes of instructions and for the fundamental operations (Basics); i.e. fail, general unification, bind, trail, dereference and decdr, as well as for the microcode as a whole.

Benchmarks	Performance (KLIPS)			
	Baseline Data (1)	No Prefetch (2)	Prefetch Unit (3)	Prefetch + Buffers (4)
concat	239.4	171.4	204.2	176.1
naive reverse	231.7	172.9	202.4	173.1
quicksort	137.3	112.6	129.3	96.3
serialize	131.2	108.0	123.4	94.9
differen	85.7	57.6	77.4	58.7
query	166.6	131.5	149.4	117.6
queens	138.4	119.4	135.4	103.0
mumath	136.5	110.8	126.3	98.6
circuit	97.1	81.7	91.7	67.7
Average	151.5	118.4	137.7	109.6

Table 5.12: The Effect of the Prefetch Unit

Measured	Frequency of Use (%)							
	Instruction Classes							Total
Qty	Proc	Indx	Cls	Get	Put	Unify	Basic	
1. States								
Count	44	41	81	29	43	89	148	475
%	9	9	17	6	9	19	31	
2. Busses								
(%)								
T	16	5	5	31	21	18	20	16
T1	43	0	2	14	16	26	11	15
MDR	18	15	9	21	33	16	25	21
R	16	29	12	41	15	22	22	21
3. Func								
Units(%)								
ALU	27	39	23	41	16	33	26	30
Memory	75	27	62	45	65	46	43	51
4. Parallel								
Busses(%)								
0	30	66	77	41	44	42	43	52
1	52	20	19	31	37	36	39	36
2	14	15	5	10	19	21	17	15
3	5	0	0	14	0	1	1	2
4	0	0	0	3	0	0	0	0.2
5. Brnching								
(%)								
P-branch	9	20	9	14	5	29	13	16
M-branch	7	24	12	31	23	20	17	20
Branch	16	44	21	41	28	43	26	33

Table 5.13: Static Microcode Statistics

The first section of the table shows the breakdown in number of states and percentage for each instruction class. The largest fraction of states is dedicated to the fundamental operations. In particular, the processor state restoring operation of the fail microroutine and the unification of compound terms in the general unifier account for most of the states in this column. The unify instruction class uses a significant fraction of the total as two microroutines are provided for each instruction for read and write mode. The get instruction class is anamously low since these instructions often use the general unifier, bind and trail microroutines. The large fraction of states allocated to the clause control class is primarily due to the **escape** instruction and its function of communicating with the host to pass operands and receive results.

More interesting data is shown in the next two sections of Table 5.13. Here the percentage of states in each column utilizing the four major busses (T, T1, MDR, and R) and the ALU and the path to memory are shown. More than half of the states involve a memory operation. The data shows that the processor busses are underutilized; only about one state in five makes use of one of these busses. This suggests that tighter microcode can be written for the PLM.

The underutilization of busses is more evident in the next section of Table 5.13 where the percentage of states in each column using 0, 1, 2, 3, or 4 busses simultaneously is shown. Over half of the microstates use no busses (ALU and memory operations and microbranching do not show up in this data). A majority of the remaining states make use of only a single bus. Only one state in the microcode makes use of all four busses in parallel.

Besides data transfers and ALU and memory operations, the other function performed in a microstate is branching. The last section of Table 5.13 shows the percentage of states in each column which include a microbranch. Data is provided for any form of branch, and specifically for P-branching and M-branching. Here again, underutilization of the microarchitecture is evident in that only one state in three branches. Form the data it can be seen that only 10% of states that contain a branch contain both a P-branch and an M-branch.

The underutilization of the features of the microarchitecture suggested in the static analysis of microcode is born out with a dynamic study. Table 5.14 shows the percentage of cycles executed for each benchmark which make use of the four major busses and the ALU and path to memory. It is interesting to note that the utilization of the T-T1 bus pair (average 41.2%), representing the data access stage of instruction execution, is higher than the MDR-R bus pair (average 24%), representing the put away stage of instruction execution, in the dynamic case where in the static case the reverse is true (21% for MDR-R, 15.5% for T-T1). This is due to the fact that where a microroutine has few common entry points (utilizing T-T1 to access operands) it has multiple exit points (utilizing MDR-R to put away results).

The overall effect of the underutilization of resources in the microcode is manifest in the Instruction Cycle Count (ICC), i.e. the average number of cycles executed per instruction. The dynamic data available from the simulator allowed the ICC to be calculated. The results are shown in Table 5.15. Also shown are the average memory operations per instruction and the average number of cycles per memory operation. For the current microcode an average of 7 cycles per instruction are executed. This is partially due to the state saving and restoring operations involved in backtracking. However, even the deterministic benchmarks have an average ICC of 4.9 cycles. For the non-deterministic benchmarks, sidetracking can reduce the ICC by saving and restoring less state, but sidetracking cannot be applied in all cases. For the benchmarks to which sidetracking was applied, the ICC was reduced on average by only 13.5%.

The memory operation data presented in Table 5.15 shows that the ICC of the PLM is not blocked by memory operations. On

Bmk	Frequency of Use (%)					
	T	T1	R	MDR	Mem	ALU
concat	41	48	29	17	35	36
n-reverse	38	45	29	21	33	33
quicksort	38	46	23	21	46	37
differen	39	55	28	17	44	38
serialize	39	44	25	22	41	47
query	30	42	32	25	38	49
circuit	37	44	19	32	49	35
queens	37	38	16	29	50	32
mumath	38	44	22	27	47	33
browse	39	42	20	25	50	33
Average	37.6	44.8	24.3	23.6	43.3	37.3

Table 5.14: Dynamic Bus Utilization

Benchmark	ICC (cycles)	Memory per Instruction	Cycles per Memory
concat	4.4	0.73	6.1
naive reverse	5.2	0.90	5.8
quicksort	7.2	2.4	3.0
serialize	7.3	2.0	3.6
differen	6.4	2.0	3.2
query	7.5	2.3	3.3
queens	8.9	2.3	3.3
mumath	7.1	2.4	2.9
circuit	8.8	3.9	2.7
browse	7.4	2.5	2.9
Average	7.0	2.2	3.6

Table 5.15: ICC and Dynamic Memory Statistics

average, every 3.6 cycles a memory operation is done. Alternately, an average of 2.2 memory operations are performed per instruction. This suggests that for this instruction set, an ICC of between 3 and 4 cycles per instructions should be possible. This represents a factor of 2 performance gain over the current microcode.

FURTHER IMPROVEMENTS TO THE PLM

Form the analysis of the previous section, several areas for improvement in the PLM are evident.

(1) *Dereference and detrail.* These two operations are responsible for extending the ICC of many instructions. For example, the cycle count for **get_list** in write mode was shown to be 13 cycles. Of these, 4 cycles were

dereference and 5 cycles were for the trail check operation. With better bus utilization, dereference can be done in 2 cycles and for **get_list**, a trail check can be done in parallel with the other instruction transfers. This results in 6 cycles for **get_list**, a savings of over 50%. Similar techniques can be applied to other unification instructions. An alternate trail mechanism is discussed below.

(2) *Instruction prefetch.* An early design decision in the PLM was to share the Memory-Data bus for access to memory, prefetching instructions from the Instruction Buffer, and for updating the P register in jump instructions (new-P). Such a scheme reduces the number of connector pins between boards in the hardware. While this is not a particularly critical problem in a TTL implementation, it is important for a VLSI implementation to reduce the number of pins for the chip (c.f. Srini [55]). However, this shared bus reduces the opportunities for parallelism in microcode, particularly at the instruction boundary where a prefetch and an memory write may be required. In these cases, extra states were added to microroutines to avoid a bus collision. Table 5.16 shows the percentage of states executed which used the Memory-Data bus for data, prefetch, and new-P operations. By providing a separate bus for prefetch, the Memory-Data bus contention can be reduced by 35% thus enabling a reduction of the ICC of many instructions.

(3) *Top of Stack calculation.* In the PLM the top of the Stack is indicated by either the E or B register. If an environment is at the top of the Stack, an E+N calculation must be done. Additional hardware and data path could be provided to compare E and B, add E and N, and gate either B or E+N to the MAR based on the comparison results for those instructions needing the top of the Stack. Such an enhancement could reduce the two or three cycles required

Benchmark	Frequency of Use (%)			
	for Data	for Prefetch	for New-P	Total
concat	16	16	2	35
naive reverse	17	14	2	33
quicksort	31	14	1	46
differen	28	15	1	44
serialize	26	14	1	41
circuit	24	11	3	38
query	35	12	1	49
queens	36	12	2	50
mumath	32	13	2	47
browse	34	14	2	50
Average	28.1	13.5	1.7	43.3

Table 5.16: MEMDAT bus Utilization

to get the top of Stack address to the MAR in the current implementation to a single cycle.

(4) *Y register address calculation.* Likewise, many of the data manipulation instructions require the calculation of the address in the environment of a Y register operand by adding E and the register specifier. An additional data path modification can produce this address in the MAR in a single cycle rather than two cycles.

(5) *An improved trail mechanism.* Whenever variables are bound in the PLM, a decision must be made as to whether to trail the binding. This decision involves a comparison of the variable location to various registers in the machine, an operation which can take up to five cycles. Additional

hardware can be provided to continuously perform these comparisons in parallel to indicate when a trail operation is to be performed.

(6)   *Extended tag support.* The hardware tag support in the PLM is restricted to the primary tag bits and the cdr bit. Extended tag support to include secondary tag bits could provide added support for built-in processing. A secondary tag branch mechanism would also simplify the instrucitons dealing with NIL.

CHAPTER SUMMARY

This Chapter has described a set of experiments using the level 2 simulator for evaluating the performance of the PLM. A discussion of the experimental paradigm used in the design of the PLM was provided. The level 1 and level 2 simulators were then described as well as the benchmark programs and measurements used in the experiment. The experiment tests included:

(1)   A case study of the determinate concat benchmark. This study showed how, using only compiler techniques, the performance for concat can be improved. The techniques described, however, are not restricted to determinate concat but may be applied to many Prolog programs if sufficient information is available to the compiler.

(2)   An analysis of cdr-coding in the PLM. Cdr-coding was found to be effective in improving both time and space requirements for list processing in some instances. The modified cdr-coding scheme suggested in this Chapter was shown to be equivalent to a non-cdr-coded implementation in its worse case and superior otherwise.

(3)   The effects of environment trimming. Environment trimming was found to be not very effective in reducing Stack space requirements and was shown to have a detrimental effect on performance.

(4)   The effect of sidetracking. The technique of sidetracking introduced in Chapter 3 was studied and found to be very effective in improving performance for non-determinate benchmarks while also providing gains in determinate cases.

(5)   The effect of host speed. A study was conducted on the effects of both host processing speed and memory access time on the performance of the PLM. PLM performance was shown to be strongly effected by these two parameters. The results for host processing of built-ins suggested that the functional unit of the PLM should be enhanced to allow more internal built-in processing.

(6)   The effect of buffers and caches. The buffers and caches provided in the design of the PLM were analysed and found to be effective in mitigating the performance losses for non-ideal memory systems.

(7)   A critique of the PLM microcode. The findings from both a static and dynamic analysis of the microcode showed that the current microcode does not effectively utilize the parallelism available in the microarchitecture.

Finally, several areas for improvement of the PLM to further enhance its performance advantage were discussed.

From the results of the tests described in this Chapter, it can bee seen that, while the PLM provides respectable performance for Prolog, an additional factor of from 2 to 3 is not unreasonable to expect.

CHAPTER 6

CONCLUSIONS

The previous chapters have developed a CISC architecture for the efficient execution of Prolog programs. The model for Prolog execution discussed in Chapter 1 was shown in Chapter 2 to be efficiently implemented by a concise, high level instruction set for an abstract machine proposed by Warren. In Chapter 3 extensions to the instruction set were proposed to provide the complete functionality of the Prolog language. Enhancements to both existing instructions and to the execution model were also proposed to improve performance. Chapter 4 proposed a microarchitecture for implementing the abstract machine and described its realization in hardware. Finally, Chapter 5 discussed the quantitative affects of the features of the PLM on performance. This Chapter summarizes the contributions of this research and provides direction for future work.

The major contributions made in this book are:

(1)   *Implementation of the Prolog **cut** operation.* Two instructions, a state bit, and a modification of the environment frame were proposed and shown to implement the search tree pruning effect of the Prolog *cut*. The nature of *cut* in a purely AND sequence of subgoals of a clause and within a disjunction was shown to be different and thus required different treatment. The mechanisms of the **cut** and **cutd** instructions were also shown to be sufficient to implement variations on the cut operations such as "snips" and hard and soft cuts.

(2)   *Improvement of clause indexing mechanisms.* A very simple scheme for hashing constant and structure data was

proposed to implement the clause filtering effect of the **switch_on_constant** and **switch_on_structure** instructions of the WAM. A modification of the semantics of these instructions allowed a uniform method for compiling procedure code to include the creation of a single choice point for a procedure.

(3)   *An escape mechanism for implementing built-ins.* An **escape** instruction was added to the instruction set to provide the facility to perform the built-in predicates of Prolog in the loosely-coupled coprocessor environment of the PLM. Three classes of built-ins were defined; compiler implemented built-ins using existing instructions, internal built-ins executed by the functional units of the PLM under microcode control, and external built-ins executed by the host processor communicating through shared memory. An analysis of the effects of built-in processing speed showed the need for strong support in the PLM for internal built-ins for overall high system performance.

(4)   *A scheme for* **assert** *and* **retract** *in compiled code.* The *assert* and *retract* built-in support for program modification in Prolog was described as a combination of compiler, run-time library, and external support. Three mechanisms were proposed; a fast *assert*, low run-time performance method for short lived clauses, an expensive *assert*, efficient run-time performance method for long lived clauses, and a median method for instances in between. A fourth mechanism was also described for side-effect variables commonly implemented via *assert* and *retract* in Prolog.

(5)   *A cdr-coded implementation of compound terms.* The representation of Prolog compound terms (lists and structures) using a cdr-coding scheme was proposed and implemented in the PLM. The scheme requires the addition of a new instruction, **unify_cdr**, and a new fundamental

operation **decdr**. It was shown that cdr-coding provides for more space efficient and can provided more time efficient processing of compound terms.

(6)   *A sidetracking mechanism.* An alternate form of back-tracking, termed sidetracking, was introduced. The side-tracking technique provides the facility to create choice points with a reduced amount of state information and a subsequent failure operation which backtracks to alternate clauses without restoring state. Such a mechanism was shown to be effective in improving the performance of tail recursive procedures and in preventing the repetition of work performed during head unification when "guards" are employed in procedures to discriminate clause selection. Significant performance enhancements were demonstrated for benchmarks for which sidetracking could be applied.

(7)   *Hardware tag support.* Hardware tag support is a major contributor to the superior performance of the PLM for symbolic processing. Specialized data paths for construct-ing and processing tagged data items and specialized microbranching on tags from various registers throughout the processor allowed the microcode to implement the instruction set in an efficient form.

(8)   *Specialized buffers and caches.* The memory bandwidth problem is particularly acute for symbolic languages such as Prolog. A sophisticated Prefetch Unit minimized Code Space access and a Write Buffer for Data Space access were shown to be effective in improving performance. A simple cache scheme for a single choice point was also proposed to further assist in the time consuming operation of saving and restoring state for backtracking.

DIRECTIONS FOR FUTURE RESEARCH

The PLM is but one implementation in one style of processor design (loosely-coupled CISC coprocessor) of an architecture for Prolog. The field of specialized processors for symbolic computing is still young and much remains to be done. The lessons learned in designing and implementing the PLM have suggested many areas for improvement and continued research. Some ideas have been presented in Chapter 5 and others are provided here.

(1) *Pipelining*. The PLM achieves parallelism at the microarchitecture level by static scheduling of transfers in the microcode. With this method, no overlap of instructions is realized. Pipelining the stages in the execution of each instruction and overlapping successive instructions is a potential source of improved performance.

(2) *Caches*. The use of caches in the memory hierarchy is a technique well studied and applied in conventional processors [53]. Further studies of the memory reference behavior of Prolog such as those of Tick [58]), are required to design effective caches for a Prolog architecture.

(3) *Extend sidetracking*. Sidetracking, as it was described here, has some limitations on its applications. For example, during head unification, variables which are bound and trailed may need to be unbound on backtracking. Since the short fail operation of sidetracking does not detrail, it may not be used in such instances. One variant on sidetracking could optionally detrail as well. The possibilities of many variants on partial fail operations is open for further study.

(4) *Improved compiler technology*. Prolog compiler technology is still in its infancy. Areas such as interclausal interactions and the use of mode declarations may provide mechanisms for more optimal code. In particular, automatic detection of sidetracking opportunities and its implementation are strongly dependent on modes and cross-clause information. Van Roy etal. [62] have described additional methods for utilizing mode information for compiling Prolog for a modified WAM engine. Early work on static and dynamic mode generation has

also begun (c.f. Chang [10], and Hermenegildo [28]).

(5)   *Additional coprocessors.* Additional tightly coupled coprocessors can extend the functional capabilities of the PLM without interfereing with its symbolic processing operations. Such a collection of different processing styles may enhance the built-in processing performance of the PLM and may allow tighter integration of logical, functional and procedural languages and programming styles.

CONCLUSIONS

The combined effects of the techniques and mechanisms described in this book have produced an architecture for Prolog which meets the ten fold improvement in performance set as the goal of this book. Table 6.1 shows the execution times, in milliseconds, for a set of benchmark programs proposed by Warren. The first two columns show the results for interpreted and compiled Prolog derived by Warren [63]. The third column shows the projected performance of the specialized hardware system, the PLM. The last column in the table shows the performance factor for the PLM over the Warren DEC-10 implementation. However, as time progresses and conventional processor technology improves, the gap narrows. For example, at this writing Quintus Prolog [3], a compiler implementation base on the WAM and running on general purpose processors, runs the naive reverse benchmark in 10.2 milliseconds on a SUN 3/160 workstation, a factor of only 3.6 advantage for the PLM. BIM Prolog [4], another compiler implementation of the WAM, runs the quicksort benchmark in 32 milliseconds on a VAX 11/785; an advantage of a factor of 5.1 for the PLM. However, with the suggested improvements discussed in Chapter 5 and with improved implementation technology (i.e. higher clock speeds), it can be seen that the PLM can maintain its 10:1 advantage by improving its performance by an additional factor of from 2 to 4. Enhancements described in the last section can further boost performance.

As an experiment, the PLM was a success both in realizing its goal of producing a high performance Prolog processor in hardware and in opening new areas of research for further study.

Benchmark	Execution Time (msec)			Factor
	Prolog-10I Interpreter	Prolog-10 Compiler	PLM Machine	PLM vs Compiler
nrev1	1160	53.7	2.87	18.7
qs4	1344	75.0	6.33	11.9
serialize				
palin25	602	40.2	3.39	11.9
differen				
times10	76.2	3.00		
divide10	84.4	2.94		
log10	49.2	1.92		
ops8	63.7	2.24		
	273.5	10.10	1.12	9.0
query	8888	185	24.3	7.6
Average				11.8

Table 6.1: Comparison with Warren's results

BIBLIOGRAPHY

1. , *Symbolics 3600 Technical Summary,* Symbolics Inc., Cambridge, MA (1983).

2. , *NCR/32 General Information,* NCR Corp., Dayton, Ohio (1983).

3. , *Quintus Prolog User's Guide,* Quintus Computer Systems, Inc., Mountain View, Ca. (April 1986).

4. , *BIM_Prolog Manual,* BIM, Everberg, Belgium (1986).

5. Barrow, H. G., "Proving the Correctness of Digital Hardware Designs," *Proc. A.A.A.I.,* pp. 17-53 (August 1983).

6. Bobrow, D.G. and Clark, D.W., "Compact Encodings of List Structure," *ACM Transactions on Programming Languages and System* **1**(2) pp. 266-286 (1979).

7. Borriello, G., Cherenson, A., Danzig, P., and Nelson, M., "Special or General-Purpose Hardware for Prolog: A Comparison," Technical Report UCB/CSD 87/314, University of California, Berkeley, Ca. (1987).

8. Buetner, K., "Fast Decompilation of Compiled Prolog Clauses," *Third International Conference on Logic Programming,* pp. 663-670 (July 1986).

9. Bundy, A. and Welham, B., "Using Meta-Level Inference for Selective Application of Multiple Rewrite Rule Sets in Algebraic Manipulation," *A.I Journal,* (16)(1981).

207

10. Chang, J-H, "High Performance Execution of Prolog Programs Based on a Static Data Dependency Analysis," Techical Report UCB/CSD 86/263, University of California, Berkeley, Ca. (October 1985).

11. Chikayama, T., Yokota, M., and Hattori, T., "Fifth Generation Kernal Language," *Proceedings of the Logic Programming Conference*, (1983).

12. Church, A., "The Calculi of Lambda Conversion," *Annals of Mathematical Study* 6Princeton University Press, (1941).

13. Clocksin, W. F. and Mellish, C. S., *Programming in Prolog*, Springer-Verlag, New York, N. Y. (1981).

14. Colmerauer, A., Kanoui, H., and Caneghem, M. van, *Etude et Realization d'un System Prolog*, Groupe de Researche en Intelligence Artificielle, Univ. d'Aix-Marseille, Luminy (1979).

15. Dahlby, S. H., Henry, G. G., Reynolds, D. N., and Taylor, P. T., "The IBM System/38: A High Level Machine," *IBM System/38 Technical Developments*, pp. 47-50 (1978).

16. Despain, Alvin M., "Notes on Computer Architecture for High Performance," pp. 59-138 in *New Computer Architectures*, ed. J. Tiberghien,, London (1984).

17. Despain, A. M. and Patt, Y. N., "The Aquarius Project," *Digest of Papers, COMPCON Spring 1984*, pp. 364-367 IEEE Press, (Spring 1984).

18. Despain, A. M., "A High Performance Prolog Coprocessor," *Proceedings WESCON 85*, (September, 1985).

19. Despain, A. M. and Patt, Y. N., "Aquarius - A High Performance Computing System for Symbolic/Numeric Applications," *Digest of Papers of COMPCON Spring '85*, pp. 376-382 (Feb. 1985).

20. Dobry, Tep, "PLM Simulator Reference Manual," Technical Note, Computer Science Division, UCB (July 1984).

21. Dobry, T.P., Patt, Y.N., and Despain, A.M., "Design Decisions Influencing the Microarchitecture For A Prolog Machine," *MICRO 17 Proceedings*, (Oct. 1984).

22. Dobry, T. P., Despain, Alvin M., and Patt, Yale N., "Performance Studies of a Prolog Machine Architecture," *Conf. Proceedings of the 12th Annual International Symposium on Computer Architecture*, pp. 180-190 (June 1985).

23. Emden, M. H. van, "An Interpreting Algorithm for Prolog Programs," *Proc. First International Logic Programming Conf.*, pp. 56-64 Faculte des Sciences de Luminy, (Sept. 1982).

24. Feigenbaum, Edward A. and McCorduck, Pamela, *The Fifth Generation: Artificial Intelligence and Japan's Computer Challenge*, Addison Wesley Publishing Co., Reading, Mass. (1983).

25. Green, C., "Application of Theorem Proving to Problem Solving," *Proc. ILACI*, pp. 219-239 (1969).

26. Griswold, R. E., Poage, J. F., and Pononsky, I. P., *The SNOBOL 4 Programming Language,* Prentice Hall (1968,1971).

27. Hansen, W.J., "Compact List Representation: Definition, Garbage Collection and System Implementation," *Communications of the ACM* **12(9)** pp. 499-507 (1969).

28. Hermenegildo, M. V., "An Abstract Machine Based Execution Model for Computer Architecture Design and Efficient Implementation of Logic Programs in Parallel," Ph. D. Thesis, University of Texas, Austin, Tx. (August 1986).

29. Hill, Dwight D. and Roy, Shaibal, "PROLOG in CMOS Circuit Design," *Digest of Papers, IEEE Spring COMPCON*, (Feb. 1985).

30. Hill, M., Eggers, S., Larus, J., Taylor, G., Adams, G., Bose, B. K., Gibson, G., Hansen, P., Keller, J., Kong, S., Lee, C., Pendleton, J., Ritchie, S., Wood, D., Zorn, B., Hilfinger, P., Hodges, D., Katz, R., Ousterhout, J., and Patterson, D.,

"Design Decisions in SPUR," *Computer* **19**(11)(November 1986).

31. Hughes, K., "Cuts and Snips," *Prolog Digest* **3**(16)(8 April 1985).

32. Katevenis, M., "Reduced Instruction Set Computer Architectures for VLSI," Technical Report UCB/CSD 84/141, University of California, Berkeley, Ca. (1984).

33. Kernighan, B. W. and Ritchie, D. M., *The C Programming Language,* Prentice Hall (1978).

34. Kowalski,, "Predicate Logic as a Programming Language," *Proceedings of IFIP*, pp. 569-579 (1974).

35. Kowalski, Robert A., *Logic for Problem Solving,* North-Holland, N.Y. (1979).

36. Kowalski, R. A., "Algorithm = Logic + Control," *CACM* **22**(7) pp. 424-436 (July 1979).

37. Li, K. and Hudak, P., "A New List Compaction Model," *Software: Practice and Experience* **16**(2) pp. 145-163 (Feb 1986).

38. McCarthy, J., Abrahams, P. W., Edwards, D. J., Hart, T. P., and Levin, M. I., *LISP 1.5 Programmer's Manual*, (1965).

39. McCarthy, J., "Recursive Functions of Symbol Expressions and Their Computation by Machine," *Communications of the ACM* **3**(4) pp. 184-194 (April 1960).

40. Mcgeer, P., Bush, B., Cheng, G., and Despain, A. M., "The ASP Silicon Compiler," *Proceedings ICCD*, (to appear October 1987).

41. Moon, D.A., "Symbolics Architecture," *Computer* **20**(1) pp. 43-52 (January 1987).

42. Nakajima, K., Nakashima, H., Yokota, M., Taki, K., Uchida, S., Nishikawa, H., Yamamoto, A., and Mitsui, M., "Evaluation of PSI Micro-Interpreter," *Proceedings COMPCON 1985*, (1985).

43. Newell, Allen and Simon, Herbert A., "Computer Science as Empirical Inquiry: Symbols and Search," *Comm. ACM* **19**(3) pp. 113-126 (Mar 1976).

44. Nilsson, N. J., *Principles of Artificial Intelligence,* Tioga Publishing Co., Palo Alto, Ca. (1980).

45. Noshokawa, H., Yokota, M., Yamamoto, A., Taki, K., and Uchida, S., "The Personal Sequential Inference Machine (PSI): Its Design Philosophy and Machine Architecture," *Logic Programming Workshop 1983*, pp. 53-73 Universidade Nova de Lisboa, (June 1983).

46. Onai, Rikio, Shimizu, Hajime, Masuda, Kanae, and Aso, Miritoshi, "Analysis of Sequential Prolog Programs," *Journal of Logic Programming* **2** pp. 119-141 (1986).

47. Patterson, D. A. and Séquin, C. H., "RISC I: A Reduced Intstruction VLSI Computer," *ARCH8*, pp. 443-457 (May 1981).

48. Perieria, F., "CProlog Users Manual, Version 1.5," Technical Report 82/11, EdCAAD, University of Edinburgh (February 1984).

49. Ratcliffe, M. and Robert, P., "The Static Analysis of Prolog Programs," Technical Report CA-11, Euproean Computer-Industry Reaserch Centre, Munich, West Germany (October 1985).

50. Robinson, J. A., "A Machine Oriented Logic Based on the Resolution Principle," *JACM* **12**(1) pp. 23-41 (Jan. 1965).

51. Roussel, P., *Definition et traitement de L'egalite formelle en Demonstration Automatique,* U. E. R. de Luminy (1972). These

52. Siewiorek, Daniel P., Bell, C. Gordon, and Newell, Allen, *Computer Structures: Principles and Examples,* McGraw-Hill, New York (1982).

53. Smith, Alan Jay, "Cache Memories," *Computing Surveys* **14**(3) pp. 473-530 (September, 1982).

54. Smith, W. R. and Rice, R., "SYMBOL - A Major Departure from Classic Software," *Proceedings AFIPS Spring Joint Computer Conference*, pp. 575-587 (1971).

55. Srini, V.P., Tam, J., Nguyen, T., Chen, C., Wei, A., Testa, J., Patt, Y. N., and Despain, A. M., "VLSI Implementation of a Prolog Processor," *Proceeding of 1987 Stanford VLSI Conference*, (March 1987).

56. Sussman, G. J., Holloway, J., Steele, G. L., and Bell, A., "Scheme-79 - LISP on a Chip," *Computer* **14**(7) pp. 10-21 (July 1981).

57. Tick, Evan and Warren, David, "Towards a Pipelined Processor," Tech. Report, SRI A.I. Center, Menlo Park, Ca. (Aug. 1983).

58. Tick, Evan, "Prolog Memory-Reference Behavior," *Technical Report No. 85-281*, SRI International, (September 1985).

59. Tomasulo, R. M., "An Efficient Algorithm for Exloiting Multiple Arithmetic   Units," *IBM J. Res. Dev.* **11**(1) pp. 25-33 (1967).

60. Ungar, D., "The Design and Evaluation of a High Performance Smalltalk System," Technical Report UCB/CSD 86/287, University of California, Berkeley, Ca. (1986).

61. VanRoy, P., "A Prolog Compiler for the PLM," Masters Thesis, University of California, Berkeley (August 21, 1984).

62. VanRoy, P., Demoen, B., and Willems, Y., "Improving the Execution Speed of Compiled Prolog with Modes, Clause Selection, and Determinism," *Proceedings TAPSOFT*, pp. 111-125 (1987).

63. Warren, D. H. D., "Applied Logic - Its Use and Implementation as Programming Tool," Ph.D. Thesis, Univ. Edinburgh,

Scotland (1977). Available as Tech. Note 290, AI Center, SRI International

64. Warren, D. H. D., "An Abstract Prolog Instruction Set," Technical Note 309, Artificial Intelligence Center, Computer Science and Technology Division, SRI, Menlo Park, C. A. (Oct. 1983).

65. Williams, Robert, "A Prolog Machine Memory Interface for a NCR32 Microcomputer," Masters Report, University of California, Berkeley, Ca. (July 1984).

INDEX

A register 29,94
access predicate 110
access stage 132
allocate 40
assert predicate 109,202
atomic predicate 106
AX register 30
   tagging of 140

B register 29,150
backtracking 33
baseline model 159
benchmark set 160
benchmarks,determinate/
   nondeterminate 179
bind
   operation 56
   protocol 50
   rules 51,56
branch prediction 127
buffers 186
built-in predicates 105
   compiler 105
   external 105,107,139
   internal 105,107

caches 186,203,204
call 39
car 25
cdr 25
cdr field 141
cdr-bit 66
cdr-coded 17,68,202
   support for 74
   effects of 168
cdr-compressed 69
cdr-expanded 70
choice point 29
   short 100,102
choice point cache 149,188
clause code 32,39
Clause control instructions 32
clause predicate 109
Code Space 25
   modification of 117
communication area 108
compiler 93,204
concat benchmark 161
   list copy 164
   sidetracking 163
cons cell 67
constant block 37
coprocessor 205

loosely coupled 15,108
tightly coupled 14
CP register 27
cut 149
  instruction 78,80
  operation 78,201
  soft 84
cut flag 80
cutd 83

data path 130
Data Space 25
data types
  compound 24,66
  constant 23,64
  reference 23,64
deallocate 40
decdr 203
  operation 75,138
dereference 50,138,196
detrail 49,196
disjunction 82

environment 29
  size 87
  trimming,effect of 175
environment buffer 151
escape 108,139,183,202
execute 40
execute stage 132

fail operation 129,149
  short 102
failure 49

failure address 29,34,36

garbage collect bit 141
garbage collection 64
Get instructions 32,42
get_constant 43
get_list 43,169
get_nil 43
get_structure 43
get_value 43,105
get_variable 42

H register 27
hardware implementation 156
hashing 89
HB register 27
Heap 25,27,33
host processor speed 181

ICC 194
if-then-else 82,106
IFETCH 137
indexing 201
Indexing instructions 32
inference 161
instruction boundary protocol 145
instruction decode 128
instruction format 71,126
interrupt capability 136

jump instructions 127

keysort predicate 107

last call optimization 40
library routines 106
LISP 2,25
LISP machines 16
list 25
list block 37
list predicate 106
list-based representation 67
local variable 31

M-branching 136
memory access speed 181
memory reference classes 146
microarchitecture 125
microcode
    call and return 138
    conditional call 140
    critique 190
    delayed branch 133,137
    forced microbranch 135
microengine 133
mode bit 137
mode,arguement 104

N register 88
NCR 9300 156
nonvar predicate 106
not predicate 106

opcode format 71

P register 26,126
P-branching 139
PDL 26,29,59,132

permanent variable 29
pipeline 132,204
prefetch 137,144,197,203
prefetch unit 126,189
problem solving 10
procedure code 32,37,90
Procedure control instructions 32
proceed 40
processor state 136
Prolog 3
Prolog model 3
PSI 16
Put instructions 32,42
put-away stage 132
put_constant 44
put_list 44
put_nil 44
put_structure 44
put_unsafe_value 44
put_unsafe_variable 87
put_value 44
put_variable 44

read mode 31
repeat predicate 106
retract predicate 109,111,202
retry 36,149
retry_me_else 104

S register 28146
search tree 6,10,96
secondary tag 66
set predicate 110
side-effect variables 109

sidetracking 100,163,203,204
  for head unification 104
  for tail recursion 102
  effects of 178
simulation 11
simulator
  level2 158
  level 1 157
sort predicate 107
SPUR 18
Stack 25,28
structure 24
structure block 37
structure predicate 106
structure-based representation 66
switch_on_constant 36,89
switch_on_structure 36,89
switch_on_term 36,88,105

tag bits 64
tag data path 144
tag support 199,203
tagged architecture 23
tagged data, construction 141
tail recursion 95
Tail recursion optimization 40
temporary register 30
top of stack 197
TR register 29
Trail 25,29
trail
  operation 56,138,198
  rule 57
trust 36,149

trust_me_else 85
try 33,35,149
try-block 90
try_me_else 34

unification 58
unification mode 31
Unify instrucitons 32,42
unify operation 58
unify predicate 105
unify_cdr 74,77,202
unify_constant 46
unify_local_value 46,86
unify_nil 46
unify_value 46
unify_variable 45
unsafe variable 27,44,86

var predicate 106
variable binding 50
variable block 37

Warren Abstract Machine 23
Warren,David 23
write buffer 148,188,203
write mode 31

Xenologic X-1 156

Y register 29,145,151,198